the COMEBACK KIDS

THREE ANIMALS WHO OVERCAME THE IMPOSSIBLE

POTATO

ANGEL

BUELLER

BY AUBRE ANDRUS

SCHOLASTIC INC.

Photo credits: Cover (top left): © Iowa Farm Sanctuary; cover (top right): © Lindsey Taylor; cover (bottom): © Holly Azzara; title page (left): © Iowa Farm Sanctuary; title page (center): © Holly Azzara; title page (right): © Lindsey Taylor; page 5: © Iowa Farm Sanctuary; page 81: © Holly Azzara; page 167: © Lindsey Taylor; photo insert pages 1–6: © Iowa Farm Sanctuary; photo insert pages 7–11: © Holly Azzara; photo insert pages 12–13: © The Dodo; photo insert page 14: © Lindsey Taylor; photo insert page 15 (top): © The Dodo; photo insert page 15 (bottom): © Lindsey Taylor; photo insert page 16: © Lindsey Taylor

ISBN 978-1-338-69268-6

10 9 8 7 6 5 4 3 2 1   22 23 24 25 26

Printed in the U.S.A.   40

First printing 2022

Book design by Veronica Mang

CONTENTS

INTRODUCTION

WHAT DO A NEWBORN ZEBU, A Munchkin cat, and a bulldog puppy have in common? They're three animals who overcame the impossible!

Angel the calf couldn't even stand weeks after she was born on a miniature zebu farm. Luckily, she found a new home at Shawn and Jered's sanctuary filled with misfit animals. Her recovery didn't go as planned, but it ended up being even better than her new owners could have imagined. Now Angel gets around just fine—in her own special way. As an indoor pet cow, she's definitely unique!

Potato, an especially tiny Munchkin cat, was born with a body so small that it caused a lot of health issues. The shelter that rescued her was afraid she'd never get adopted. But they never could have guessed that she'd become a social media star and thousands of people would fall in love with her! After a few close calls and a serious surgery, her recovery amazed everyone—especially her new owner, Holly.

Bueller, a bulldog puppy, was given to a shelter because his weak legs made it impossible for him to walk. His foster family helped heal him faster than anyone could have predicted—and they found him the perfect forever home after a difficult search. It turned out that Bueller came into Lindsey and Alex's home at just the right time, and he went on to heal the hearts of his new owners in a big way.

Angel, Potato, and Bueller's comebacks took a lot of time, love, and hard work. It wasn't easy, and it wasn't always fun. But it was worth it in the end. Young or old, big or small, two legs or four—these three inspiring true stories show that with a little love and kindness, we can get through even the biggest challenges.

ANGEL'S STORY

ANGEL

CHAPTER 1

THE RESCUE

SHAWN OPENED THE DOOR OF THE truck as they pulled up to the farm. She jumped out before it had even stopped moving. Her bright blonde hair swung in a high ponytail as she jogged toward the green fenced-in pasture just ahead. Her husband, Jered, parked the truck, then followed closely behind her. They had both been on farms plenty of times before, but this wasn't your everyday farm—it was a farm for zebus, a type of small cattle from Asia.

A little zebu calf was sitting in the grass near the fence. Shawn immediately bent down to pet her. She almost didn't even notice the farmer and his wife standing nearby. Tears were already streaming down Shawn's face. She couldn't wait to bring this calf home.

"She's the size of a newborn puppy," Shawn said in awe as she lovingly hugged her newest rescue for the first time. She had never seen a zebu up close. She couldn't believe how cute this calf was. She looked like a little fawn, but instead of being brown like a baby deer, she was black and white spotted. Two tiny horns sprouted from the top of her head. A few teeth poked out of the bottom of her adorable smile. Her ears were perked up, and she was wearing a bandanna around her neck. At first glance, it seemed like she was a healthy little calf just sitting in the grass. But the reality was that her back legs were tucked permanently underneath her body. They were twiglike and wouldn't straighten out like her front legs. The farmer, Bob, told Shawn and Jered how happy and sweet this little calf was, even though she couldn't stand up. That's why they named her Angel.

"Hi, Angel," Shawn said as she pet her gently.

Tracey was watching from a window in her parents' farmhouse. Her mom and dad stood in the front yard near the pasture, with Angel resting just in front of them. Shawn and Jered were sitting in the grass petting her. So *this* was the couple that Tracey had heard so much about. Tracey had assumed the people who ran the animal rescue would be older, like her parents. But Shawn and Jered looked so young! She had been told that Iowa Farm Sanctuary could change the lives of animals in need. That's exactly why she had called them to her parents' farm. This calf needed a miracle.

Tracey felt so relieved watching the couple interact with Angel as she walked out the front door to greet them. She could already tell that Jered and Shawn would give this calf the extra care and attention she needed. Just days before, Tracey had thought there was no hope for her. Her dad, Bob, raised miniature zebus and other animals on this farm. In all his years of raising zebus, he had never seen one like Angel. When her back legs didn't begin to straighten on their own after she was born, he took her to the vet. The veterinarian thought that her leg muscles just needed to be massaged and straightened every day. But that didn't work.

The vet then realized that the calf's condition was more serious: Angel was born with her two back kneecaps in the wrong places, so she'd never be able to stand. It was like her back legs were locked in a bent position. The veterinarian recommended putting Angel to sleep, but Tracey asked her dad to let her find someone who could raise Angel and give her the extra care she needed. Bob loved the calf, and he wholeheartedly agreed that she deserved to find a new home.

Tracey had been thrilled when she found a forever home for Angel at a sanctuary in Florida. Florida had the perfect kind of weather for zebus—nice and warm. The new family planned to drive from Florida to Tracey's parents' farm in Illinois to pick up Angel. But then the call came in:

"I'm sorry, we can't. We just don't have room for her."

Tracey was shocked. The new owners had backed out at the last minute. Where would this little zebu live now? Bob had done everything he could to help Angel in the two months since she had been born, including doing stretching exercises with her four times a day. He even carried her inside to feed her a bottle whenever she was hungry, since she couldn't stand up to nurse from her mother. But Angel was growing and Bob was getting older. He wouldn't be able to lift this little calf forever. If she couldn't stand, he couldn't take care of her.

Tracey had had to start the search for a new home again—and fast. Thankfully, she found Shawn and Jered at Iowa Farm Sanctuary, and they had answered her call for help immediately.

And now they were here to take Angel to her new home.

Tracey introduced herself to the couple. Jered was bearded with tattooed arms and his long dark blond hair was tied back in a low bun. Up close, she could now see that Shawn had a cow tattoo on her leg. Shawn was watching the other zebus grazing far away, inside the pasture. But one of the zebus had broken away from the pack. The lone zebu started walking toward them. She reached the fence, then started bellowing loudly as Shawn picked up Angel gently.

"That's her mom," Tracey explained.

"I think she's saying good-bye to Angel," Shawn said.

Tracey agreed. She knew that Angel's mom understood what was going on. As much as possible, Bob would set Angel next to her mom's pen so they could be close to each other. But Angel couldn't safely stay inside with her all the time. Since Angel couldn't move around on her own, her mom might accidentally step on her and hurt her. But they still loved to spend time together when they could.

Once, when Angel was sitting near her mom, a large male zebu (called a bull) came near them. Angel started bellowing at him as loud as she could. For being so little, she had no fear! Tracey didn't know what Angel said to that bull, but she had *something* to say, and she wasn't afraid to say it. That was when Tracey knew that Angel would be able to protect herself—with or without her mom nearby.

Angel would need that feistiness now that she was leaving the farm to live at a new place. Bob handed over Angel's remaining powdered milk to Shawn and Jered, and Tracey gave them some extra supplies. Because Angel couldn't stand, she needed to lie on a clean disposable pad. It had to be replaced frequently to keep her clean so she didn't develop sores on her skin every time she went to the bathroom.

It was a good thing Tracey was a nurse (for humans). When she learned that a calf at her parents' farm needed extra help, she had brought over supplies to keep the calf healthy. She had fallen in love with Angel on day one. But now Tracey had to walk away. She was too sad to say good-bye to Angel. As she stepped back inside the house, she cried. She would miss Angel and all of her little zebu kisses. Tracey watched from the window as Jered and Shawn, with Angel in her arms, stepped back into their truck. Tracey knew that Angel had a tough road ahead of her, but she'd have a great life at Iowa Farm

Sanctuary, where she could get the extra attention she needed.

The truck pulled down the road and drove off into the warm September afternoon.

Angel gave one last look toward her barn. Her mom had said good-bye, and then the nice humans were crying. Now she was sitting in someone's lap, and they were moving quickly through the fields and away from her farm. Angel did the one thing she knew how to do: give kisses, which was basically licking someone's face. That was her way of saying hello and thank you. She wasn't quite sure what was going on, but she had a feeling that these humans were going to do something good for her.

CHAPTER 2

THE MISFITS

IT WAS ALMOST A THREE-HOUR drive from the miniature zebu farm in Illinois to Iowa Farm Sanctuary in Marengo, Iowa. Shawn was so glad they had said yes to rescuing Angel. When the message came in that a zebu in Illinois needed help, Shawn and Jered's first concern was that they didn't have room for another large animal. But once Angel's owners sent a photo, their concern vanished. The calf was so tiny! They hadn't realized she was a miniature zebu—and an especially small one at that. Newborn miniature zebus are usually twenty-five pounds when they're born. Angel was only twenty-two pounds—and she was already two months old.

Shawn and Jered hoped that Angel would be able to walk one day. They planned for the little zebu to live in their "misfit barn." Iowa Farm Sanctuary had two barns: one for the rescues who were healthy and independent, and the other for animals who didn't quite fit in with the rest of the herd, like Ellie. Ellie was a happy black cow who had been surrendered to the sanctuary because she was born blind, but Shawn and Jered could tell that something else was wrong, too. When they took her to the veterinarian, they discovered that Ellie had a really bad infection in one of her legs that required surgery. It was a very dangerous procedure, but Ellie's leg healed perfectly. Her recovery blew Shawn and Jered away. Ellie had overcome so much at such a young age.

Pumpkin was another member of the misfit barn. She was a cow who had been given to the sanctuary by a young girl named Grace. Grace knew that her cow was sick and was having trouble breathing; she needed help. Grace was sad about giving up her cow, but she was happy to know she could visit her again soon at the sanctuary. When Shawn and Jered took Pumpkin to the veterinarian, they discovered that Pumpkin had scarring on her lungs from being sick when she was younger. Pumpkin would likely always have a loud cough, but she could go on to live a happy life. Now the cow loved running across the pastures at top speed.

You would never know she once had trouble breathing!

When these two misfits first met each other, something amazing had happened: Pumpkin became Ellie's "seeing-eye cow"! Pumpkin knew Ellie couldn't see, so she would guide her around the barn and pasture—and if Ellie ever got lost, she could find Pumpkin again by listening for her loud cough! The two made a great team, and they soon became best friends, too. Pumpkin was sassy and sweet: She knew that Ellie relied on her, and she even let Ellie suckle on her ear for comfort—though it was kind of annoying.

It had taken a lot of time and energy to make sure these two cows could live their best lives. Other people might have given up because it was too much work, or simply because they didn't know what to do. But Shawn and Jered were more than willing to give animals like Ellie and Pumpkin extra love and care. They couldn't wait to learn Angel's quirks, habits, and favorite things. They knew this was the first day of a long journey, but it was one they were happy to be on.

As Angel slept in her lap on the drive back, Shawn kept thinking of Isaac, a white goat with black ears and black legs. He had arrived at Iowa Farm Sanctuary just four months ago from a petting zoo in Missouri. He was born with legs that were similar to Angel's—but it was his front legs that looked like they were locked in a bent position. When he was two months old, he was basically walking on his elbows. After they took Isaac to their favorite veterinarian at Iowa State University, they learned that nothing was wrong with his bones—it was the tendons and ligaments that held his bones together that needed to be strengthened. If he wore splints on his front legs, he would be able to walk. That was great news to Shawn and Jered, even though it meant Isaac needed to wear the splints for the rest of his life.

Every day, Shawn and Jered had put on Isaac's splints. Twelve hours on. Twelve hours off. Then, one month later, when they took Isaac's splints off, he stood up on his own. "Oh wow!" Shawn had said. "Let's leave these splints off for an extra twelve hours and see what happens." Isaac never needed the splints again. He ran around like a happy, healthy goat now. You'd never know that just a few months before he couldn't even stand up.

Shawn hoped a happy ending like this awaited Angel. She was constantly amazed by the rescued animal residents at Iowa Farm Sanctuary. They'd taught her so much. Isaac,

Pumpkin, and Ellie reminded her and Jered every day that they could overcome any obstacle, even if things were hard at first. That's what would get them through Angel's journey, no matter what direction it took.

CHAPTER 3

ONE STEP FORWARD

SHAWN SET ANGEL DOWN IN A room full of straw with bowls of grain and water. Angel sat still and looked back at Shawn. Minutes passed, but Angel didn't move an inch. She was sitting exactly where Shawn had placed her. *She really can't move at all,* Shawn thought. Isaac the goat had been able to army crawl to his food and water. But this zebu was stuck in place. Shawn brought the bowl of grain and water closer. There was no way she could leave this zebu alone.

"Can she just come inside?" Shawn asked Jered.

They usually didn't bring farm animals into their house. The house was for humans and smaller animals like cats and dogs. But Jered agreed. They couldn't leave this zebu out in the barn by herself. However, they were both worried that their dogs, including the Great Danes, Davey and Leif, wouldn't like a new animal suddenly appearing in the house. Davey was friendly, but Leif didn't get along with everyone. They carried Angel inside, nervous to see what would happen.

What was going on? Angel was being carried into a room with two furry things running toward her. She leaned in closer to the nice lady who was holding her. *Don't set me down!* These furry things weren't quite like anything she had seen before, and they were bigger than her and barking. Then there was a little black-and-white fluffy thing who ran away, too. One of the big furry things came closer to her. Angel wasn't used to this!

Angel jumped a bit when she saw the dogs run down the stairs. Bob had warned Shawn and Jered that mini zebus were pretty jumpy and easily startled. Their black-and-white cat, Jet, ran away from all the commotion. But Davey immediately pranced over and gave the calf a few sniffs.

"She's so harmless; I think the dogs can sense that," Jered said. "Davey's a gentle giant, anyway."

Leif looked the zebu over. He didn't seem to mind the new arrival, either.

"Angel and Leif are more alike than they are different," Shawn added. She knew all animals, whether they were farm animals or house pets, were just the same. They were all so loving and emotional. Shawn looked at Angel. The little calf was so sweet and trusting. Of course she was—she'd relied on people to carry her around since she was born, and knew they were there to help her. Shawn gave her a big hug.

Later that night, Jered left for work. As a paramedic who helped sick or injured people in emergencies, he often worked the night shift. Shawn carried Angel up to her bedroom and set her on their bed.

"You'll sleep with me tonight, Angel," she said. Bowls of grain and water were nearby, and Shawn had a full bottle of milk ready to go. Angel would have to be bottle-fed around the clock. As soon as the zebu saw the bottle, she perked up. Milk was her favorite thing in the world.

"Oh, look at that milk mustache," Shawn said as she fed Angel.

Shawn never imagined that one day she'd be sleeping side by side with a baby zebu. But here she was cuddling a puppy-sized cow. This was the best day ever.

Iowa Farm Sanctuary had tens of thousands of followers on social media. Those followers loved seeing photos of new rescues and reading updates on animals who were recovering from an illness or injury. Shawn and Jered were grateful for the support of so many people. Not only did their followers cheer on each of their rescues, but they also donated money to help keep the sanctuary running. Shawn was excited to share their latest arrival first thing the next morning:

"RESCUE ALERT: Meet Angel! Angel is a mini zebu calf, about two months old, who has never been able to walk. Despite all their efforts, Angel's family was running out of options as she grew and grew. We're so thankful they found us, and we are honored to get the opportunity to change this sweet girl's life, see her run and play, and do normal calf things. Please check out Angel's photos and find it in your heart to donate a few bucks to her care. Stay tuned for updates!"

Their followers fell in love with Angel right away, just as Shawn and Jered had. Soon, the comments were pouring in.

"She is so cute! I love those two little teeth sticking out!"

"Welcome, sweet Angel!"

"Oh, how I want to cuddle her!"

"My heart just exploded!"

"Oh my goodness! She looks like she has a wig on!"

Shawn was willing to do whatever it took to get Angel to walk: leg braces, splints, surgery, massages, physical therapy. And it seemed like Iowa Farm Sanctuary's followers agreed. They had donated over one thousand dollars to help Angel. Shawn's heart warmed knowing that there were so many others out there who loved animals as much as she did. She could already tell that Angel was going to be one of the most popular residents at the sanctuary.

It was raining outside. Jered was back from work, and Shawn was in the living room with Angel. Angel had propped up her front legs and was sitting up like a dog. Angel had only been living with them for one day, but Shawn had never seen her do that before. Then Angel tried to scoot forward, but it wasn't easy. Her bottom was dragging on the ground. Shawn didn't know what to do. Should she stop her? Should she help? On a whim, she grabbed Angel's back end and lifted it into the air. Before Shawn knew what was happening, Angel started stepping forward slowly with her front legs. Then her little front legs started moving fast!

Finally! Someone had given her just what she needed—a little lift! That's all Angel had wanted. She stepped with one leg, and then the other, and then again and again and again. This was so fun! She could go over here and over there. And, hey, where did those other furry animals go? And where's my grain? Ooh, there it is. Let me run to it!

"She's walking!" Shawn said.

Jered rushed over to see the calf running around the living room, and Shawn bent over uncomfortably trying to keep up with her.

"Well, now we know that she has that fight in her!" Jered said. "She wants to run, and she has the energy to do it."

Shawn was laughing as she followed the little zebu around the house. Occasionally, Angel would try to buck, which means she'd jump up with her head and the front part of her body because she was excited.

"Let's get this on camera," Shawn said. She let Jered take a turn supporting Angel while she filmed a video on her phone. Angel looked so cute in her yellow bandanna and her light blue diaper. Jered was holding up her back end and Angel was prancing around the rug in circles, looking happy as can be. It was as if she knew how to walk, even though she'd never done it before.

"You can see her back legs taking steps as best they can," Shawn said. "She loves feeling mobile!"

Jered set Angel down.

"We should get her a cart," he said with a smile.

Shawn looked disappointed.

"I think the cart will be a setback for Angel," Shawn said. She wanted Angel to be able to walk like Isaac—on all four legs. She thought that a cart would just slow down her recovery process. Angel's first vet appointment was tomorrow, and in Shawn's eyes, a cart was the worst-case scenario. Shawn wanted Angel to enjoy walking through the pasture in the warm sun and running alongside the other barn animals one day—that's what was natural to her. A cart would help her walk, but Shawn wanted her to be able to run independently like the other animals could. They'd just have to see what the doctors said.

CHAPTER 4

ONE STEP BACK

SHAWN LOOKED OVER AT ANGEL, who was sitting calmly in a laundry basket filled with soft blankets. The laundry basket was buckled safely onto the front seat of the truck, and they were on their way to the Iowa State University Large Animal Hospital. Even though Angel was small, her breed was classified as a large animal. This was where Shawn took all of her farm animal rescues, so the hour-and-a-half drive had become familiar.

Shawn drove past corn and soybean fields. Red barns with dairy cows, turkeys, chickens, and pigs. The view out her window reminded her how different her life was from just a few years ago.

Back then, Shawn and Jered had lived in Iowa City, and the idea of opening their own animal sanctuary outside the city was nothing but a dream. They knew that the first thing they would have to do was buy a farm. But all of the farms for sale in the area were huge. Farming was very popular in Iowa, and most farmers had tons of animals with many barns and pastures. Shawn and Jered were looking for a smaller farm where they could care for animals in need. After months of searching, they finally found a house with two barns and a pasture for horses.

They were so eager to buy the property and move in that they told the owners to just leave their horses in the pasture! They didn't mind caring for them until the owners found a new farm.

Shawn and Jered had dreamed of opening a sanctuary because there were a lot of farm animals who needed help in Iowa. Sometimes animals got injured falling off a truck as they were moved from one farm to another. Other times, farmers didn't have time to care for a sick or injured animal. Now Iowa Farm Sanctuary was there to rescue any farm animal in need.

The first two residents at Iowa Farm Sanctuary were piglet runts named Monkey and Marley. As the tiniest piglets in their litter, they wouldn't grow as fast or as big as their siblings, so a farm employee took them in and helped raise them. But she couldn't keep them forever.

She discovered Iowa Farm Sanctuary and brought the little runts to Shawn and Jered. They were thrilled to take in these two piglets as their first official rescues. And things took off from there. From the moment their sanctuary opened, people were reaching out for help. Now about half of their rescues came from nearby farmers.

Jered and Shawn had a hard time saying no to anyone. It didn't take long before the two barns at the sanctuary were almost completely full. At this moment, Iowa Farm Sanctuary was home to more than forty rescued animals. Some were big farm animals, like cows and pigs, and some were smaller animals, like chickens, ducks, and the friendly black barn cat, Batman. The way Shawn saw it, there was no difference between a cat and a cow. Farm animals and pets had so much in common. Why love one animal and not the other? She believed in treating everyone with love and respect, regardless of whether you were human, furry, or feathered. And she didn't expect anything in return. Animals were her friends, and she was happy to help.

Large animal hospitals were different from human hospitals. Instead of polished white hallways and clean rooms for the patients, there were stalls with hay on the ground filled with animal patients like cows and horses. But the hospital provided the same kind of amazing care that a human hospital would. These doctors just applied their knowledge to animals instead.

Shawn watched nervously as the vet took her first look at Angel.

"I think the best-case scenario is that we can get her a cart," she said.

Shawn was shocked. They hadn't even taken X-rays yet. This couldn't be right.

"I was hoping she'd be like Isaac the goat," Shawn said. "Things looked bad for him at first, but he learned how to walk very quickly."

"I can tell upon first sight that surgery or splints won't be an option this time," the vet explained.

Angel was supposed to stay at the hospital for at least a few days while they observed her and came up with a plan. Shawn hadn't expected to get bad news so quickly. The veterinarian told Shawn that they'd still move forward with X-rays and a checkup just to make sure, but she was very confident that this animal would never be able to walk on her own. Shawn was heartbroken.

Later that night, the animal hospital called to confirm the news.

"Her legs are in a locked position, and a cart is the best option," the vet said. "We'll start working on training her in a cart immediately."

"I understand," Shawn said reluctantly.

"In the future, we may have to amputate her back legs if she gets really large and her legs start causing her pain."

Removing her back legs? This was the complete opposite of what Shawn had dreamed of for Angel's future. And how would the little calf buck upward if she was strapped to a heavy cart with rolling back wheels? Despite her disappointment, Shawn knew Angel was in excellent hands at the Iowa State University Large Animal Hospital. They planned to transfer Angel from the large animal wing to the small animal section and fit her with a cart that was originally meant for a dog. The veterinary team would work with Angel to get her used to the cart and then call up Shawn and Jered when Angel was ready to go home. The little zebu would have to stay there for at least a week.

When Shawn and Jered rescued Angel, it had been the best day ever. But now Shawn was feeling overwhelmed by the vet's news. The past two days had been a roller coaster of emotions.

"What are we going to do with this calf?" Shawn asked.

"Well," Jered said as he took in all the news and thought about their options. "Angel might have to permanently live in our house."

A housebound cow? Had there ever been such a thing?

CHAPTER 5

ROLLING RIGHT ALONG

IT HAD BEEN FOUR DAYS SINCE Angel's appointment. But it was time for Shawn to update their followers on the zebu's situation. It wasn't the update she had hoped to share, but she wanted to remain positive for Angel. The zebu *would* be able to walk one day. She would just need the help of a cart to do it.

"After careful examination and research, the

team at the ISU Large Animal Hospital has determined that Angel is not a candidate for surgery. We will be looking at cart options to help her gain mobility—she so wants to run and play!" Then Shawn asked if anyone would be willing to donate toward Angel's vet bills and new cart. The comments and the love poured in—as well as almost four hundred dollars within thirty minutes.

"I just want to cuddle her!"

"You are her angels."

"Happy to contribute to this sweet critter."

"She is too cute for words."

Like Shawn, their followers were disappointed to hear that Angel's recovery wouldn't be the same as Isaac's. But their well wishes gave Shawn and Jered hope. Every animal who lived at Iowa Farm Sanctuary had a great life. And Angel would, too, whether she walked on all four legs or rolled with a cart. Shawn and Jered had so much love to give and a great community of supporters behind them. By the end of the day, almost nine hundred dollars had been raised for Angel, and an anonymous donor agreed to pledge another four hundred dollars. People were kind. Kindness is what would carry them through this.

Angel's front legs were straight. But her bottom wasn't sitting on the floor. It was propped up by a pink thing with two black wheels. The doctors were calling to her. She was standing in the middle of a walkway, and the other animals in the pens on either side of it were watching. She didn't really know what she was supposed to do. But then she thought of that time that the nice lady had picked up her back end and she ran around the house. She took a step forward. The rest of her body followed. She took another step. The rest of her body followed again. Hey, this was kind of cool! Step, step, roll, step, step, roll. She could get used to this!

It had been a few days, but Shawn and Jered finally got a great update from the veterinarians at the animal hospital. They sent over a video of Angel happily rolling around in her new pink cart.

"She's a natural," Shawn said. "Look at her go!"

Shawn and Jered had tears in their eyes watching their little zebu prance through the concrete hallways of the animal hospital. Her yellow bandanna. Her pink cart. Her black and white spots. She was the cutest little zebu they had ever seen. After a twelve-day hospital stay, they finally got approval from the doctors to pick her up. They shared the update with their followers.

"It's the best day ever! Angel is coming home! Since she's a growing girl, we're renting a cart to help her get around for the time being. She's a natural at walking with the cart. Our hearts soar to see her so happy!"

Again, the sanctuary's followers replied with tons of support.

"I can't wait to come meet her."

"I love those little teeth! She's starting to smile!"

"It will be so fun to see her tootling around in her cart at the farm."

"Angel is so adorable."

The veterinarians assured Shawn and Jered that Angel could use the cart safely and without pain. Her back legs stayed in their natural tucked position as she rolled. It didn't require any effort for her to keep them up. With practice, her front legs would keep growing stronger. Angel was going to be an active calf after all.

Shawn had thought the cart would be a setback. But now she knew that nothing would be a setback for this zebu. They couldn't wait to get her home.

CHAPTER 6

OLD FRIENDS

"ALL RIGHT, ANGEL," SHAWN SAID. "Let's get you in your cart."

Angel's cart was made for dogs, so it didn't fit her perfectly. A zebu's body isn't shaped the same as a dog's body. For example, Angel had udders that got in the way of the chest harness. That's something a dog doesn't have to worry about! But the veterinarians at the hospital had shown Shawn and Jered how to adjust the cart so that it fit Angel the best way possible. There were lots of straps and screws and adjustments that could be made as she grew bigger. Shawn and Jered decided to rent the cart for now. Angel was a growing calf, which meant they'd have to replace it in a few months. Eventually, they'd get her a custom cart, but not until she was done growing.

Seeing Angel walking in her cart was exciting and terrifying at the same time. Jered and Shawn couldn't turn their backs on her; otherwise, she might tip over. With practice, her front legs would get stronger. But for now, they were so frail that they were afraid she'd hurt herself. To get Angel into the cart, one person had to hold her while the other person held the cart. But Jered and Shawn wouldn't always be home together, so they'd have to figure out how to get her into the cart by themselves at some point. That would be a challenge.

Angel could only stay in her cart for about an hour and a half before she got tired. Jered and Shawn had already figured out the signs she gave when she was ready to be taken out of her wheels. She'd roll backward into the wall or couch, which would lock her back wheels into place and relieve her body of some of the pressure. So as soon as she started backing up, they'd take her out and set her onto one of her soft beds with a pee pad underneath. They changed those frequently to make sure she always had a clean bed.

Shawn and Jered watched the little zebu roll up to a coffee table so she could do her grain puzzle. It was a teal, rectangular tray with red and white boxes inside. She had to push off the lids of each box to find the grain hidden inside.

She loved it. Then she rolled around the living room some more.

"She's so proud of herself," Jered said.

"And so are we!" Shawn added.

Shawn thought of all the people who had cheered them on and donated money. *Amazing things can happen when we work together for a more compassionate world,* she thought.

Angel was rolling around the living room happily until she heard a *chop chop* noise. She stopped rolling. What was that? Was that what she thought it was? *Moo! Moo!* Angel could tell that there were yummy vegetables being cut up in the kitchen, and she wanted some—now. She rolled her pink cart up to her human mom. *Moo! Moo!* She wasn't going to stop until she had a piece of broccoli in her mouth. *Moo!*

"You don't sound like a lady when you do that!" Shawn said.

When Angel first moved in with Shawn and Jered months ago, she had been quiet and timid. But now she rolled and mooed around the house like she owned the place! She was very comfortable in her new job as Shawn and Jered's pet cow. In fact, she had turned into a total diva. If she heard a knife cutting vegetables, she wouldn't stop mooing until she got some as a treat. And any time Leif and Davey were fed their dog food, Angel demanded a treat, too.

"She went from a well-mannered calf to a demanding little dog," Jered said.

Moo! Angel continued.

"Before she was a docile, sweet little princess,"

Shawn said as she gave her some broccoli.

Most zebus lived outside, but Angel was loving her "inside family" right now. There was Shawn, Jered, Davey, Leif, and Jet the cat. Angel loved to lick Jet's ears. Jet just lay there and tolerated it. So did Davey. Angel loved to lick his ears, too, especially when the two of them were cuddled together on the couch with the fireplace roaring nearby. Sometimes when Angel snuggled with Davey, she'd stare off into the distance with squinted eyes and make a snoring noise. But she was awake! The snoring noise just meant that she was happy. It was a weird zebu thing that Shawn and Jered loved. Because Angel and Davey had become such great friends, they slept on the same king-sized bed together every night. They just loved to cuddle. Shawn wasn't sure if Angel thought Davey was a cow. Or if Angel thought that she was a dog. But it didn't matter to these two friends.

Iowa Farm Sanctuary was open to the public on Sundays all year round, except during the winter months. Kids and families would come by to pet the rescue animals and give them treats from the sanctuary's Garden for Good, which was where Shawn and Jered tried to grow a lot of the food they fed to the animals. Today they had some extra-special visitors: Tracey and her parents were coming to see how Angel was doing in her new home. Usually, visitors weren't allowed to walk into the white house with the red roof that Jered and Shawn called home. But they'd made an exception today!

"Oh my god, that's so adorable!" Tracey said. When Tracey stepped inside Jered and Shawn's house, she saw Angel sitting in a playpen wearing a light blue diaper. It was a playpen meant for human babies, but it was the perfect place for Angel to rest. "Look at you, Miss Fancy Pants!"

Shawn and Jered took out the pink cart. Tracey and her parents watched as they gently lowered the little zebu inside. They had to carefully slip her bent back legs into position and tighten a few straps. Angel immediately wheeled down the hallway to Tracey, then to each of Tracey's parents like she was saying "Hi." Then she gave them lots of kisses, just like she had months ago.

"You sweet little girl," Tracey said to her as she happily accepted the zebu kisses she had missed so much.

"She's using the cart really well," Bob said. "She knows exactly what she's doing."

Bob watched Angel wheel around the house

like she had been born with wheels. When her back wheel got stuck on the corner of a chair or another obstacle, she knew to take a few steps backward to unstick her wheel, and then she'd glide forward again without a problem. Back at the farm, Bob took care of Angel's mother and her three siblings every day. It was so amazing to see that this little calf who once couldn't walk was almost as active as the other three calves back home.

"She's like a human little girl," Tracey said to Shawn and Jered. "She's like, 'I know I'm cute and I'm spoiled!'"

Tracey was thrilled. She could tell Angel was so happy at the sanctuary. And she could tell how much Shawn and Jered loved her. Even when she was talking to Tracey, Shawn would lovingly keep her eyes on Angel. Then Angel would wheel over. She was like a magnet to Shawn. *You can tell that's who she's the closest to*, Tracey thought. Tracey believed that although animals can't speak, their body language would tell you whether or not they'd been treated right. And she could tell that Angel was being treated like a princess. Shawn was like a mother hen protecting her baby. It warmed Tracey's heart.

Later that day, Shawn waved good-bye to Tracey and her family as they pulled out of the sanctuary's drive and back onto the highway. She turned and watched the other visiting families interacting with the rescued animals in the pastures beyond the two white barns. She hoped one day soon Angel would be able to join those animals. But since she was still so small and because her wheels weren't very steady on bumpy ground or mud, she couldn't run freely with the herd just yet. It wouldn't be fair or safe to throw her in there with all the larger animals yet.

Shawn carried Angel to a patch of grass and sat with her. The big trees on their property covered the two of them with shade. Angel was propped up in her lap and they watched Pumpkin and Ellie walk around the pasture. Shawn imagined Angel rolling through the grass with the two of them one day. As she pet the little calf, she wondered what Angel was thinking. Did she wish she could walk in the pasture, too? Maybe Angel didn't know any different. Maybe it didn't break Angel's heart. But it broke Shawn's.

CHAPTER 7

NEW FRIENDS

"OH, HI! THANKS FOR THE KISSES," Jered said as Angel sat in the bathtub. "A little spa day for you."

"Seeing a cow in a bathtub might seem strange to other people, but it's totally normal around here," Shawn said. This was just another Saturday night at their house.

Angel needed daily warm bubble baths

because she sat down so much. She would develop sores on her skin if she wasn't cleaned properly. Shawn used to give Angel those baths, but now Jered had taken over bath duty.

"She's almost doubled in size," Jered said as he lifted her out of the tub and began drying her off.

"She's getting heavy!" Shawn agreed.

Angel now weighed seventy pounds. Shawn had a hard time carrying her up the stairs or into the bathtub, and even getting her into her cart. In fact, Angel almost didn't fit into her cart anymore. They'd have to do something about that soon. A cart was the only way Angel could get exercise. They wanted to keep the little calf active and let her enjoy her independence. If the cart was too small or uncomfortable, she wouldn't want to use it. Maybe this time they could get something designed especially for

Angel's body. It would be expensive, but it would be worth it. It was pretty clear that this zebu was going to live a mostly housebound life.

There was a foot of snow on the ground. Angel hadn't been outside in almost two months. It was too cold, and her wheels were not meant for snow. But like everyone, Angel was getting antsy. She wanted fresh air. Today she finally got to go outside—but not with her wheels. Jered carried her through the winter cold and set her in the front seat of the car. They were on their way to the animal hospital again. This time they were going to get a customized cart that would be perfect for Angel's body shape. It would be fully adjustable so that she could continue to grow into it.

"My hope is that we can get her into a cart

that's a little bit taller, so she's in more of a normal position," Dr. Joe, a veterinarian at the animal hospital, said as he examined Angel, who was lying on a bed of hay. A veterinarian assistant was helping him with Angel, and another one was taking notes. Dr. Joe adjusted his glasses with his blue-gloved hand as he explained the plan to Shawn. He agreed that if they kept Angel in her current cart, it would get too uncomfortable and she would probably want to stop using it. Everyone's goal was for Angel to remain active. And a new cart was the only way to do that.

"She looks strong," he added, happy to see what a bright little zebu she had blossomed into.

With help from the veterinarian, Shawn and Jered ordered a custom cart for Angel. It would be built to match her body measurements exactly. Shawn hoped that this was the final step in Angel's journey. She hoped the new wheels would give her little zebu all the confidence she needed to not only wheel around the house, but wheel around outside, too. She wanted Angel to be able to steadily walk across the pasture and not worry about tipping over or getting in the way of the larger animals. But for now, she had to wait until the new cart arrived in one month.

"Hey, Bee-bu! Look what came today!" Jered was holding up a large blue box with a picture of three dogs on it. Each of the dogs was wearing rear wheels. "Look what we got!"

Angel looked up from her bowl of grain when she heard her nickname being called. Shawn and Jered couldn't wait to open the box. Jered pieced together all the parts: the pads, the wheels, and the pink tubes that formed the cart. Angel sat and watched while she snacked on grain. Jered was happy to see that everything could be adjusted a lot more than in her last cart. He lifted up Angel and placed her in it.

"How does that feel?" he asked her. It fit perfectly. "She seems to be a lot more comfortable."

Angel stood a little taller. She seemed like she liked it. She looked great in her pink cart and green bandanna.

Shawn agreed. "She's definitely happy."

Jered held out some broccoli to encourage her to roll forward.

"Come on, Angel!"

She took a few steps and snapped up the broccoli. The cart wheeled forward just as it should. It seemed like it fit her well! Now that a month had passed, the winter weather in Iowa was passing, too. The temperature was in the fifties today, so it was a perfect afternoon to get Angel outside in her new cart. They had a big plan: get Angel in the pasture with Pumpkin and Ellie. Jered removed Angel's green bandanna and strapped on a blue plaid cape to keep her warm.

"We're going to get them into a small pasture, give them some grass, and have them play together," Jered said, repeating the plan back to Shawn.

Angel's first obstacle was a bit of mud immediately outside the back door of the house.

"This is a bit of rough terrain here. What are you going to do?" Jered asked her.

Angel rolled right through without a problem.

"There you go! Off-roading!" Jered smiled. "You can tell right away that she is more confident getting around."

He led Angel into the pasture where Pumpkin and Ellie were waiting.

Two cows were grazing up ahead by the fence. They were much bigger than Angel. One was brown and one was black. Angel rolled across the pasture. She felt like she could move a little faster now with this new pink cart. The black cow looked up as Angel joined them, and gave her a sniff. The three of them snacked in peace for a few minutes. Then the two cows started walking around. Angel followed. The brown one came up right up to Angel. She rubbed her head against Angel's head. That made Angel feel happy. Then the black one came over and gave her a few kisses with her nose.

"There she is!" Jered said. "Aww."

When cows rub their heads together, it's a sign of affection. It seemed like Pumpkin and Ellie liked Angel! This was going even better than Shawn and Jered had expected.

"You're being so sweet. Are you going to start licking her now, Angel?" Jered laughed.

"She's like a whole new cow out there playing with Pumpkin and Ellie," Shawn said. "I think it will be great for her to spend more time with the cows outside in the sunshine, rather than being cooped up in the house all day."

"Seeing her walk through the grass and go through the mud—it's evidence of her comeback," Jered said. *It's a good feeling,* he thought to himself.

"She'll get time with the other animals who are like her outside," Shawn added. "And then she gets to come in and sleep in the luxury king-sized bed at night."

Shawn laughed. She realized that Angel was getting the best of both worlds. Every animal they rescued led them down a different path and had their own story. Angel inspired her every day. She had been born with a major setback, but she continued to surprise everyone. It made Shawn want to do anything and everything she could to help this little zebu.

Shawn had been rescuing animals since she was a kid—she had memories of feeding baby squirrels with an eyedropper with her dad's help. That's where her passion for rescuing began. As she watched Angel roll around the pasture, she felt proud of all that she had been able to do with Iowa Farm Sanctuary in such a short time. She thought of all the animals they had rescued: the piglets, Marley and Monkey, who wouldn't have lived another day on the farm, but now played happily in the sun. Isaac the goat, who once could only crawl but now walked with ease. Ellie and Pumpkin, the two struggling cows who found an incredible friendship with each other. And now Angel, the little zebu who could confidently roll anywhere with just two working legs.

There were so many other animals they had saved, too. And Shawn knew they would go on to change the lives of even more. That made it all worth it. Without Iowa Farm Sanctuary, Angel wouldn't have had her happily ever after. And neither would Shawn. She couldn't imagine a life doing anything else.

IOWA FARM SANCTUARY

Iowa Farm Sanctuary rescues farm animals who are in need of love and compassion. Cofounders Shawn and Jered Camp provide these animals a safe home where they can live the rest of their lives happily. About sixty animals call IFS home, from cows and pigs and sheep, to goats and chickens and ducks. Many of them came to the sanctuary with an illness or injury that required extra patience and care. IFS covers the costs of medical bills for veterinary visits, surgeries, medicine, and whatever else is needed to ensure a rescue animal can live a great life. But they can't do it without the help of donations and volunteers.

IFS holds Open Barn Days for families throughout most of the year. Visitors to the sanctuary, some of whom have never seen farm animals up close, can experience firsthand how smart and sweet these animals can be. Visitors can pet and feed the animals and learn more about their rescue stories.

SHAWN AND JERED'S RESCUES

Angel, Isaac, Pumpkin, and Ellie aren't the only rescues at Iowa Farm Sanctuary. There are so many animal residents, and they each have a unique personality and rescue story. Some rescues have come from zoos, some from farms, and other from homes where the owners couldn't care for them anymore. Shawn and Jered always keep an open heart and an open mind when it comes to animals in need.

GEORGE

George the pig was being transported to a new location when he fell off of a truck on the highway. Luckily, one of Shawn and Jered's friends happened to be driving by and rescued the pig on the side of the road. George recovered from his fall, and he soon formed an amazing friendship with a little piglet named Guy at Iowa Farm Sanctuary. (Guy had also fallen from a truck when he was just twenty-one days old.) The two are inseparable and even eat their meals together.

BOSWORTH

Bosworth was a pet duck who was abandoned at a city pond. He couldn't fly or defend himself against predators. Now Bosworth has found a family with the rest of the birds at the sanctuary. His favorite activity is splashing in the pond—whether it's a sunny day or a cold one. If he's not playing in the pond, Bosworth can be found looking at himself in the mirror. He's very handsome!

GERALD, WILLOW, VALENTINA, AND SNOWY

These four goats were abandoned by their mother soon after being born. Goats usually only have two babies at a time. But their mother had four babies at once, which made it hard for her to care for them all. The quadruplets— Gerald, Willow, Valentina, and Snowy—all live at Iowa Farm Sanctuary now. They had to spend a week at the Iowa State University Large Animal Hospital when they were babies, but now they're all doing well. Gerald is very protective of his brother and sisters.

MAX

Max the cow survived a terrible truck accident that occurred when he was being transported to a new location. Max had the most serious injuries of all eight cows in the accident—a broken jaw and broken bones around his right eye, which left the right side of his face paralyzed. But with help from veterinarians, he recovered and grew into the healthy, happy cow he is today. When visitors look at Max, they would never guess how much he's been through.

SUNDANCE

Sundance is a sweet brown-and-white goat who was brought to IFS by a farmer. The farmer noticed Sundance had a bad leg and needed help.

The veterinarians at Iowa State University discovered that Sunny had an infection, and his leg needed to be amputated. Now he's a three-legged goat, but he's happy as can be hanging out with the other goat residents at the sanctuary. He walks just fine—visitors sometimes don't even notice he has only three legs!

WHAT'S A MINIATURE ZEBU?

Zebus are believed to be the oldest breed of cow. They've been around for thousands of years! Zebus are originally from India. They are also known as humped cattle for the small hump that appears above their shoulders. There are seventy different types of zebu breeds, including the miniature zebu, which is the smallest breed of cow.

Miniature zebus like Angel usually stand around three and a half feet tall—that's shorter than the average kindergartener! It takes them about three years to grow to their full height. When they are first born, they are only sixteen to eighteen inches tall and weigh around twenty pounds. Newborn zebus are known for being adorable and looking more like a fawn (a baby deer) than a cow.

Zebus are most often red or gray in color, but they can also be black or spotted like Angel. Even though they may look like cows, there are many ways that zebus are different from most cows you'd see on a farm in the United States. Zebus are smaller in size, and have horns, larger ears, and a hump. Their humps are similar to camel humps and are used to store fat and nutrients.

We may not see many zebus in the US,

but they are popular around the world. In Madagascar, a country in Africa, zebus are a symbol of power and strength. They are often given as gifts and were even once used as a symbol for royalty! Today, zebus are most commonly found in Southwest Asia, Africa, Australia, and South America. That's why they are used to hot and dry weather. But they can adjust easily to other climates—Angel has sure gotten used to Iowa winters!

POTATO'S STORY

POTATO

CHAPTER 1

TINY

AS ALYSSA STARED AT THE LITTLE cat on her living room floor, all she wanted to do was to pick her up and pet her. But she knew she couldn't. This cat was special and preferred to have all four paws planted firmly on the ground. She was unlike any of the other cats and dogs Alyssa had fostered over the past six years. When you work at an animal shelter, you can't avoid taking home a few animals with you now and then! That's how the animal shelter's newest patient had ended up sitting in her house.

Alyssa grabbed a can of wet cat food and poured it onto a plate. When she turned back around, she couldn't believe her eyes: She had already forgotten how small this cat really was! Even though she was two years old, the cat was as tiny as could be. Munchkin cats like this one were known for their small size and short stumpy legs, but she was even smaller than expected. Her white fur had gray markings on it, but it had been so matted when she arrived at the shelter that they'd had to shave off a lot of it. Because her limbs were so short, she couldn't properly clean herself like a typically sized cat. That meant she needed her fur combed, her eyes wiped with a cloth daily, and her bottom cleaned after she went to the bathroom.

"Giselle is a much better name than Munchkin," she said to the little cat with a giggle. When the cat had been dropped off at the shelter a few days ago, Alyssa and her coworkers decided to change her name. She had been named Munchkin after her breed, so they knew they could come up with something more creative. Gisele was the name of a supermodel with long legs. This cat had the shortest legs they had ever seen, so it made them laugh to call her Giselle (although they spelled it a little differently). Even when she was standing up, it looked like she was lying down.

Giselle heard a click on the ground—food!—and started walking toward the yummy smell. She sniffed the ground until her nose bumped into the plate. Jackpot! She plunged her little face into the food and started licking furiously. She could get used to this. There had been a lot of loud noises and strange smells the past few days, but this new place was nice. She kept eating until there was nothing left. And then she licked the plate clean.

*   *   *
*   *   *

The morning Giselle had been surrendered to the shelter, she was having trouble breathing. Her owner knew that the cat had medical issues of some kind, but she didn't have the time or the money to properly care for her anymore. Alyssa had accepted the cat and brought her to the shelter's veterinarian, Dr. Moses, immediately.

"I don't know if we'll be able to help this cat," Alyssa said as she handed her over. Giselle's eyes and ears were twitching. She just looked sick.

Dr. Moses put an oxygen mask on her. She seemed to like it because it helped her breathe so much more easily.

Now that Giselle had been resting at Alyssa's house for a few days, she was doing a little bit better. The pain medications and antibiotics the vet gave her at her first appointment were definitely helping. But Dr. Moses still had many concerns.

The list was long. Giselle's skeleton wasn't quite right. Her organs were too big for her body, and her rib cage was too small, which was squishing her lungs and making it hard for her to breathe. Her head was too big, which was putting stress on her spine. And that wasn't all. When she had first arrived, Dr. Moses had placed the tiny cat on the floor so she could observe her behavior. Her previous owner had said that when the cat would try to groom herself, she'd get tired and fall over. During the appointment, Giselle had paced slowly and seemed disoriented. She bumped into everything. And when anyone tried to pet her, she seemed very scared. After an exam, blood tests, and X-rays, Dr. Moses called in a neurologist, which is a doctor who studies the brain, for more help.

"She can't see," the neurologist said. "She's blind."

The staff at the shelter were shocked. Giselle had eyeballs that seemed to follow everyone around the room. But her optic nerve, the part of the eye that sends images from the eyeballs to the brain, wasn't connected to her brain. That meant that her eyes reacted to light, but her brain wouldn't get those visual messages. So while she looked like she could see, she really couldn't.

That's exactly why Alyssa couldn't pick up Giselle right now, even though she wanted to. Getting picked up made the little cat dizzy. She didn't know where she was. It was also uncomfortable for her. When she was pet suddenly without a warning, it startled her. Blind pets can be easily scared. Alyssa was slowly learning what this little cat liked and disliked. She rubbed the cat's belly softly. Giselle purred. That was something new to add to the "like" list!

Alyssa was the shelter manager of the Massachusetts Society for the Prevention of Cruelty to Animals, or the MSPCA. Every year, she and her coworkers helped thousands of stray and unwanted pets in Boston find forever homes. Usually, a Munchkin cat would get adopted quickly—people liked how small they were. But Giselle was *too* small. Plus, she was blind and had a lot of other medical issues.

How would they ever find this little cat a home? Alyssa had to look on the bright side. Giselle was around two years old, so she'd already survived this long with all her special needs. Multiple veterinarians were working hard to figure out everything that was wrong with her so they could help her as much as possible. She could walk just fine. She loved to eat, particularly wet cat food. All in all—besides her health issues—she was just like a regular cat! She was affectionate and low-key; she just needed a little extra love.

Someone would see that eventually, right? Alyssa thought. But then she had an idea. If she created a special social media account for Giselle, everyone in Boston could learn about her and see through photos and videos that she was just a regular cat. Social media would be a great way to get Giselle's story out there. It was going to be tough to find her the right home. She'd need a lot of care. They needed to find the perfect person to adopt her. Someone who could be her cheerleader through the good and the bad. She also had to have the right setup: a low litter box and a safe home free of stairs and obstacles so she could walk around safely.

Alyssa logged into Instagram and started an account called @realstumpycat. *Here goes nothing,* she thought.

CHAPTER 2
SUPERSTAR

HAVE YOU SEEN THIS? **HOLLY'S BEST** friend had sent her a link. She clicked it and was taken to a social media account for a really cute cat—a really cute cat who was up for adoption.

You're the second person to send me this! Holly replied.

Earlier today, Holly had been talking to her best friend and had literally said, "I don't think

I'm ready to adopt another cat yet." Her cat, Lucy, had passed away just two months ago. Holly had adopted Lucy as an elderly cat who needed a home where she could live out the rest of her life, but losing a pet was always sad. Holly just wasn't sure if she was ready to take in someone new. Besides, she already had four other cats to take care of: Lady, Jack, Little Sister, and Olive.

So why were her friends sending her this cat now? She had *just* said she wasn't ready! But as Holly looked at the profile she noticed this cat was local. She was in Boston, like Holly was. And she needed a family to love her.

Holly was famous among her friends for her love of cats. She even had tattoos of cats! If anyone knew of a cat in need, they turned to her first. Holly tended to take in elderly cats, sick cats, or cats who had behavioral issues, like being afraid of humans.

Holly had grown up with cats. Her family had gotten their first cat when Holly was just one year old. The cat's name was Maxie. He lived to be nineteen years old, and she thought of him as her little brother. She'd always related to animals more than humans. Growing up she'd had other pets like a parakeet, an iguana, rats, and a bunny, but she always felt an extra-special love toward cats. At age fourteen, she took in her first stray, a tiny calico named Babe—who ended up being pregnant with five kittens! Holly never stopped rescuing cats after that.

She glanced down at the photo of the tiny cat one more time. Her name was Giselle. Holly would think about it.

🐾 🐾 🐾

It had been one week since Giselle arrived at the shelter. Alyssa had posted twenty photos and videos of her on Instagram. She described Giselle's medical issues and shared some cute videos of her purring and playing. It wasn't long before she realized that people loved Giselle's story. The comments were always so nice:

"What a precious little potato!"

"This kitty is so adorable."

"I love you, Giselle!"

"Her face is so sweet."

Word of Giselle traveled all over the city. *Boston* magazine wanted to share Giselle's story. Then word spread across the country. The Dodo, a digital media company that tells stories about animals, wanted to make a video about her, too. Alyssa couldn't believe how quickly the number of Giselle's followers was growing. She had originally just wanted to help get the word out that Giselle was available for adoption and raise money for some of her vet bills. But now people from all over the world were asking if they could adopt Giselle. Alyssa was getting thousands of emails. She couldn't believe it! Alyssa shared an update:

"You guys! Can you see that I'm heading big places? My foster mom says I'm getting one thousand new followers per day, and I've gotten adoption inquiries from over twenty states! I have an appointment with Dr. Moses tomorrow, and I'll hopefully be ready for a home by next week! Stay tuned . . ."

More comments followed:

"I wish I lived closer so I could adopt her!"

"Want to come live in California, Giselle?"

"We want her!"

"I'd love to adopt this precious baby."

Alyssa was overwhelmed by the messages and adoption requests. People were calling the MSPCA for more information and coming in to fill out applications. Just last Tuesday she'd thought Giselle would never get adopted. And now, only seven days later, she had *too many* people applying for her. Alyssa sent one more message letting Giselle's followers know that applications were due Friday. That was just three days away, but she had to make the deadline soon, because at this point, there were almost too many applications to read!

She also reminded everyone that they were only going to place Giselle within a two-hour drive of Boston. Because Giselle's body was fragile, transitions were hard for her—even something as simple as a car ride to the vet was difficult. Since she couldn't see, she got confused and scared when she needed to travel, which made it very difficult for her to breathe. A trip across the country would be too much for her. So, although it was nice that people around the country wanted to adopt her, Alyssa wouldn't be considering them for Giselle's new home.

After less than two weeks of posting on social media, Giselle will be adopted! Alyssa thought. At least that was the plan. She was so excited to find this special little cat a home. She watched as Giselle sat on a red plaid blanket by the fireplace. It was a cold October night and she looked so content. Alyssa had been through this process many times before. It was always hard to let go of a foster pet, but she loved seeing them find the perfect forever home.

* * *

Giselle felt warm and cozy. This was her favorite spot lately. It was quiet and calm and soft. She was allowed to lie here without being disturbed. She still wasn't quite sure where she was right now—or if she'd stay there—but she knew that people were trying to help her. Sometimes she had to be taken to other places and held by different people, which made her nervous. But at the end of the day, she was always brought back to this place, cleaned, and given food and medicine by a nice lady. Sometimes her body hurt, but right now she felt better. She drifted off to sleep to the sounds of the fire crackling softly nearby.

Holly couldn't sleep. She kept watching the videos of Giselle on social media. *Before you contact them, can you really take this on?* she asked herself. *Financially, can you take care of her? And she is* really *sick. What if she only makes it a few months?* Holly had a million questions running through her mind. But for some reason, she couldn't stop thinking about this cat.

She scrolled through Giselle's social media feed some more and then called her best friend.

"At this point, thousands of people already want to adopt her," Holly said.

"Listen," her best friend said. "Just go down to the shelter. Don't get your hopes up. Just go down there and gather information."

Her best friend was always right. Tomorrow, Holly would go to the MSPCA and learn more about Giselle.

CHAPTER 3

DECISIONS

HOLLY OPENED THE FRONT DOOR OF
the shelter and walked into a crowded waiting
room. Luckily, she didn't have to wait too long.
She was able to meet with the adoption counselor after a short wait.

She learned more about Giselle's medical
situation, and how much extra love and care she
needed. They talked about how Giselle's adopter

could make his or her home safe for a tiny, blind cat. And they discussed how to make sure Giselle had a good quality of life, which meant helping her be as happy as possible and ensuring she wasn't in pain from her medical conditions.

It was easy for Holly to talk about these kinds of things. After all, she had learned so much over many years fostering cats. She even had an entire room in her condo set up for the foster cats. She understood each animal's unique needs and could give them time and a safe space to adjust to new people and new places. All of Holly's cats went on to find forever homes, and others who she found as strays or adopted specially stayed forever with Holly as her pets. But Giselle already had a temporary safe space with Alyssa. She needed a home with someone who could take care of her for the rest of her life. So if she lived with

Holly, it would be as a permanent member of her family.

Holly began to imagine Giselle living with her, and she explained to the adoption counselor what that would look like. Holly said she'd probably keep Giselle in a special room: her office that had windows on the door and was near the couch so Holly could keep an eye on her. It was small and safe so the little blind cat wouldn't feel overwhelmed or put herself in any danger. Being self-employed, Holly had a flexible schedule and could be home often to care for her. When she wasn't home, she could easily check the cameras she had set up around the house to watch her cats. Whenever she saw a cat getting into trouble on the camera, she could easily leave work and come home to make sure everyone was okay.

As Holly talked, she began to believe that she could give Giselle the perfect home. Holly had the space, time, and knowledge to help her thrive. Maybe this was meant to be. Before she left the shelter, Holly filled out an adoption application. She hadn't even met Giselle, but she knew that she could give the little cat everything she needed, even if it required a lot of time and work. It felt like all of Holly's experiences had been leading up to this moment.

But that didn't mean the MSPCA would choose her to adopt Giselle. *Oh man, this is never going to happen,* Holly thought as she walked out of the shelter. This cat was so special, but she came with a lot of extra needs. Was Holly the right fit for Giselle? And was Giselle the right fit for Holly? Just because Holly believed so didn't mean others would see it that way. The shelter would be the one to make that decision. Holly wished she could have at least met the tiny cat, but she understood that it would have been too stressful for her. And Giselle's health was what was most important.

♣   ♣   ♣
♣   ♣   ♣

Alyssa's coworker called her over. She had just met a really nice woman who wanted to adopt Giselle. Her name was Holly, and she had a lot of experience with cats who had special needs. And most importantly, Holly wasn't interested in Giselle just because she was popular. It was something Alyssa had to consider—Giselle had eight thousand followers on social media right now, and more people were following her journey every day. The Dodo's story had been read by tens of thousands of people. Some people wanted to adopt her just because she was cute and famous, and because they were excited to run a famous social media account.

"A lot of people are in it for the glory," Alyssa

agreed. She tried to imagine what Giselle's life would be like after this. If she kept getting popular on social media, TV news shows would want her to travel to make guest appearances. Magazines and websites would want her to travel for photo shoots. Her future family could make money off her if they wanted to. But that wasn't what was best for Giselle.

Dr. Moses made it clear that whoever adopted Giselle needed to be willing to keep her protected at home. They weren't even sure how long this little cat could live based on all of her medical conditions. She needed a calm, happy, and safe environment in order to thrive. Her health had to be the number one priority for anyone who adopted her.

Alyssa looked at Holly's application and listened to more of what her coworker had to say about the interview. She knew that Holly would turn down media requests. She wouldn't take Giselle places that weren't good for her. She wouldn't treat Giselle like a prop. She would treat her like a member of her family, just as she'd done with so many wonderful cats before. And she lived just twenty minutes away.

"She's great," Alyssa agreed. "She's a good cat mom."

Alyssa looked at the stack of fifty applications she had received before the deadline. There were a lot of people she had to consider as she searched for the perfect new owner for Giselle. Was Holly the one?

"Today was the last day for applications to adopt me! Now my foster mom can focus on taking care of me and start thinking about who she will hand the reins to! I have a big recheck at the vet in a week and a half so we won't decide on my new family until then. Stay tuned!" That was the caption on the latest post on Giselle's Instagram page.

Giselle's followers were so anxious to hear who Alyssa would pick. It was a really big decision to make, so Alyssa was glad she had time to consider all of the applications while the shelter focused on Giselle's health and made sure she was 100 percent ready to be loved by a new family. Alyssa read through all the comments on the post:

"So happy there have been so many requests for her! Yay!"

"Whoever gets her will be so lucky!"

"Praying for kind and wonderful paw-rents for you, Giselle."

"SO cute! I love her! Please keep us updated!"

It was Halloween. Alyssa dressed up Giselle as a taco. Her body was wrapped in a soft yellow tortilla shell, and running down her back was a burst of glittering lettuce, peppers, and onions. She looked adorable. Alyssa shared the photo with her followers, who loved it.

That night, Giselle rested on a soft brown dog bed while Alyssa let in trick-or-treaters. Giselle's foster brother Tuna, a black-and-white dog, sat nearby. Alyssa had kept Giselle separated from Tuna the first couple weeks, but now they were getting to know each other a little. Tuna would sniff her and then walk away. He wasn't quite sure what to do with a cat who was so small.

In between giving candy to trick-or-treaters, Alyssa kept an eye on Giselle. She was pressing her little paws into the bed. Left, right, left, right.

"Are you making mini muffins again?" she asked Giselle.

Giselle loved to get cozy in soft pillows and blankets. Earlier that week, she had crawled into a gray-and-white blanket and hid so well that Alyssa almost couldn't even see her. She had been camouflaged! Now on the dog bed, Giselle sat down, then flopped over on her side to expose her belly. That meant she wanted to be scratched. Even though she couldn't see Alyssa, she knew that she was nearby. Her sense of hearing was amazing.

"You're just hammin' it up, aren't you?" Alyssa asked as she gave Giselle belly rubs.

Alyssa thought of the fifty families who wanted to adopt this sweet cat. The application deadline had been only three days ago, but Alyssa had already decided on the perfect family for Giselle. Alyssa's mind was made up. But she hadn't shared the news with Giselle's followers yet, even though they were so eager to know who would get to take the cat home. She wanted to wait until after Giselle's big vet appointment. That's where Dr. Moses would make sure Giselle was healthy enough to be adopted. Once she got the approval, Alyssa would reach out to her new family, set up the adoption, and then share the big news with everyone. She crossed her fingers one more time and silently hoped that Giselle's next appointment went well.

CHAPTER 4

EMERGENCY!

IT HAD BEEN OVER A WEEK SINCE THE adoption application deadline, and Alyssa still hadn't announced Giselle's new family. That's because Giselle's health had taken a turn for the worse. She had ended up in the emergency room just days before her big vet appointment. She was having trouble pooping, which was a sign that her digestive system wasn't working properly. This little cat was really struggling. She hadn't pooped for days. And then she'd pushed so hard that she'd strained herself. Alyssa had brought her to the animal hospital, but now they were finally home. Giselle was feeling better, and Alyssa had to send an update to her followers. She had warned them when she was on her way to the emergency room, so she knew they were all concerned about Giselle and would be waiting for some news.

"Back home from the hospital and getting a midnight snack. Thanks for all the thoughts and well wishes! My foster mom will be keeping an extra close eye on me for a while!" Alyssa wrote. Then the supportive comments started pouring in.

"Glad you are home and feeling better, baby!"

"Feel better!"

"Please take care of both of you, sweet cat and foster mom!"

"Is she okay? Sending lots of love!"

A few days later, the veterinarians at the MSPCA agreed that Giselle would need surgery soon to help her bathroom issues. Other than that, she was doing well with her current medicine and was ready to be adopted. But whoever adopted her would have to be updated on her latest medical situation, and agree to pay for the cost of her surgery. Not everyone would be willing to adopt an animal who immediately needed an expensive procedure.

Alyssa made a phone call. She was ready to notify Giselle's new mom. She hoped she'd say yes.

Holly couldn't believe it. She was on her way to Alyssa's house to meet Giselle for the first time. The little potato kitty was hers! This was great news. They decided that Holly and Giselle should meet at Alyssa's house, and then Holly could sign the adoption papers there. Since Giselle didn't love transitions like car rides and changes of environment, it was better if they didn't take her into and out of the MSPCA simply to sign some papers.

Holly drove around the corner. She was just a few driveways away from meeting her new cat! But then her phone rang:

"I'm so sorry—I have to take her to the ER," Alyssa said. Alyssa had come home from work to find the little cat struggling again. It had been days since she last went to the bathroom. "Can we reschedule? You don't need to come to the hospital with us."

"If I'm going to take care of her, let me come with you," Holly said instantly. This was her cat now. She needed to know what was going on.

"I guess you can come if you want to, but it's not going to be fun," Alyssa said.

"No, I'll come. I'll drive." Holly pulled into the driveway as Alyssa walked outside with Giselle's carrier in her arms.

Holly and Alyssa were sitting in the waiting room at the animal hospital. This wasn't how Holly imagined meeting her cat for the first time, but it was okay. All that mattered was that Giselle got the help she needed.

But Alyssa was getting concerned. Could they even adopt this cat out anymore? If she needed to go to the emergency room every few days, shouldn't Alyssa just keep her? After all, she worked at the animal shelter and had much easier access to veterinarians.

"We would feel so bad putting this on

you," Alyssa explained. "She's still so sick."

"I understand that and that's why I'm asking to adopt her," Holly said to Alyssa. Even if Giselle was sick. Even if Giselle needed surgery. Even if Giselle had to be rushed to the ER every week. Holly had only interacted with her for about thirty seconds before she was whisked away by the veterinarians. But she already knew she wanted to adopt this tiny cat. She wanted to be the one who provided Giselle with a loving, safe home.

After sitting in the waiting room for several hours, Alyssa and Holly finally got an update from the veterinarians. Giselle was doing better, but surgery probably wasn't a good idea right now. Alyssa agreed to take her home for now, and then they'd reassess whether or not Giselle was ready to be adopted.

Holly dropped off Alyssa and Giselle at

home. She wondered if she'd ever see the little potato kitty again.

As Alyssa waved good-bye to Holly's car, she felt a wave of sadness sweep over her. Not only was Alyssa worried about Giselle, but she was crushed that Holly might not get the chance to adopt her.

The pain specialist and the neurologist who were treating Giselle were going back and forth about whether or not Giselle should be adopted. They were afraid that she was too sick and might not live long enough for an adoption to make sense. But even if that was the case, Holly was the perfect cat mom. Alyssa knew it in her heart.

The next week, Holly stepped into Alyssa's kitchen. After the veterinarians had analyzed

Giselle's case yet again, they had decided: Giselle may be sick, but Holly could provide a great home for her. She'd get extra attention and love, which was just what she needed. Alyssa had called Holly immediately.

"She's as stable as she's going to get," Alyssa had said to Holly over the phone just a few days ago. "Do you feel confident taking her on? It's either you or me."

"I might as well at this point!" Holly had said.

"I don't think it's going to get any better," Alyssa had warned her.

"That's all right." Holly knew what she was getting into. And she was still willing to do it. "Let's set a date."

Now here they were signing the paperwork at Alyssa's house. Alyssa had explained all of Giselle's health issues and her daily routine of wiping her eyes, brushing her fur, and wiping her bottom. Giselle had to take two different kinds of medicine and needed four supplements added to her food. But there was still one more thing they had to talk about.

"She has eight thousand followers online," Alyssa explained, referring to Giselle's social media page. "They have been following her the entire time she's been fostered."

These followers were emotionally invested in Giselle's journey. They'd want to know who her new mom was, how she was doing in her new home, and whether she was overcoming any new obstacles that were thrown her way. Holly knew about the social media followers. But she wasn't interested in posting daily updates about Giselle. It just wasn't something that she had time for or she would enjoy doing. Plus, she wanted to focus on Giselle's health. She now had five cats to take care of. Those cats were her priority, not social media.

"I can't be someone that I'm not," Holly said. "If you want to continue to post updates, I'll send you photos and videos." Then she had an idea. "Maybe we can use her social media platform to spread awareness for other cats who are elderly or have special needs and are available for adoption."

Alyssa agreed. Once a week, Holly would send her an update and Alyssa would post it. In the meantime, Alyssa would share pictures and videos of other cats who were available for adoption at the MSPCA.

As Holly and Giselle walked out the door, Alyssa felt the same relief she felt every time one of her foster cats finally found their forever families. She was sad to see the little Munchkin cat go, but she knew she was going to a home where she would get all the love and special attention she needed.

Alyssa shared the good news with Giselle's followers:

"You guys! My mom finally made a decision about my new family. Although there were literally hundreds of wonderful, kind, amazing homes offered up, we finally narrowed it down to one home where my new mom has had tons of experience with special-needs cats, and I'll have a few kitty siblings to hopefully snuggle up with. Even though I love my foster home and I'll be very missed here, I'm super excited to settle into my forever home!"

Everyone was thrilled to learn the little stumpy potato cat had found a family. And they wanted to keep following along.

"I wish you a wonderful and healthy life."

"This is great news!"

"I hope your new kitty siblings will love you!"

"Congratulations on your new beginning, Giselle!"

Alyssa would make sure to keep sharing Giselle's journey with their followers—after all, she wanted to know how Giselle was adjusting, too! She hoped she'd see Holly and Giselle when they came into the shelter for vet visits with Dr. Moses. But mostly she wanted the next few days to go well. Her fingers were crossed that Holly didn't have to take Giselle to the hospital anytime soon. But based on her experience over the past few weeks, it was a very real possibility. In fact, it was likely. Alyssa just hoped she was wrong.

CHAPTER 5

HOME

HOLLY CAREFULLY LIFTED GISELLE from her car. The little cat was breathing heavily. She didn't like traveling in the car and not knowing where she was. But luckily, it was a short drive and they were already home. Holly couldn't wait to get Giselle inside so the cat could start getting used to her new bedroom. She opened the front door of her condo, then

Angel is a miniature zebu. When she was born, her back legs wouldn't straighten out. The farmer who raised Angel took her to the vet. There, they discovered that her two back kneecaps were in the wrong place, so Angel would never be able to walk—or even stand—on her own.

The farmer couldn't give Angel the special help she needed. Luckily, he found her a great new home at Iowa Farm Sanctuary. Angel moved to live with Shawn and Jered, who run the sanctuary.

Shawn and Jered love having Angel at the sanctuary! They help her eat and get around and spend time outside. But the best part is getting to snuggle with the little zebu!

Because Angel can't walk or stand by herself, it would be too hard for her to live out in the barn with the other rescued farm animals. Instead, Angel lives in the house with Shawn, Jered, and their dogs and cat.

Shawn and Jered carry Angel where she needs to go—including upstairs to take a bath in the tub!

After a few visits to the vet, Shawn and Jered decided that it would be best to get Angel a cart to help her get around on her own. At first, Angel wasn't so sure she wanted to try out her new wheels.

But soon, Angel was zooming around the house and the farm! The cart holds up Angel's back legs so she can walk (and roll). She loves being able to run to Shawn for a snack and visiting with the other animals.

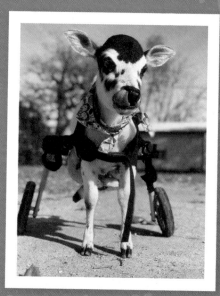

As Angel gets older, she is able to spend more time outside with the other animals. Angel loves hanging out in the pasture with two of the sanctuary's cows, Pumpkin and Ellie.

One of Angel's best friends on the farm is another miniature zebu named Harpo.

Angel is so lucky to have found such a great home at Iowa Farm Sanctuary!

All Munchkin cats are small, but **Potato** is especially tiny! This little cat has super-short legs and only weighs about three pounds. But her small size means Potato has some health problems. That's why her first owner surrendered her to the Massachusetts SPCA.

When Potato first arrived at the shelter, the vet there, Dr. Moses, shaved Potato's matted fur and put her in an oxygen mask to help her breathe. The vet also discovered that Potato was blind.

One of the shelter employees, Alyssa, decided to foster Potato while she got stronger. After many vet visits, Potato was finally ready to be adopted. She found a forever home with a woman named Holly.

Holly had lots of experience with special-needs cats like Potato, plus she had four other cats at home for Potato to play with. But Potato had to stay in a special room by herself until she got used to her new space.

But before long, Potato was right at home with Holly. She even let Holly pick her up for snuggles together on the couch!

Potato is much smaller than her cat siblings—but she doesn't let that get in the way of playtime!

Potato likes to chase the other cats, including Jack and Lady, around the house and pounce! But her siblings always know when tiny Potato needs to take a break. Then they're happy to snuggle together instead.

Potato also loves to play with her toys. Since she's blind, Potato likes toys that move or make noise, like this crinkly lobster.

But at the end of the day, nothing is better than taking a cozy nap—especially in Potato's favorite spot, right by the fire.

Potato hasn't had the easiest life, but she can rest easy now that she's found the perfect home with Holly.

Bueller the bulldog was surrendered to an animal shelter when he was just a puppy. Bueller had a condition called swimmer syndrome, which made his legs stick out to the sides instead of holding him up.

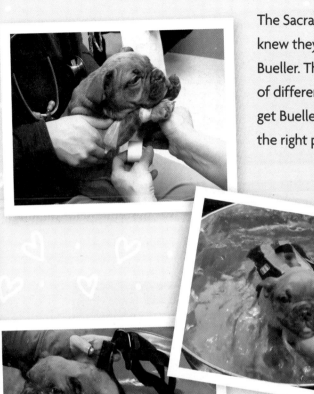

The Sacramento SPCA knew they had to help Bueller. They tried lots of different things to get Bueller's legs in the right position.

Swimming is actually a great way to help animals with swimmer syndrome! Bueller did water therapy at the SSPCA to help him learn how to hold and move his legs properly and build up his strength.

With lots of help from the vets, SSPCA employees, and his foster mom and dad, Bueller learned to walk on his own! That meant that Bueller was finally ready to find his forever home.

Bueller's new family is a couple named Lindsey and Alex. Their bulldog had passed away a few months before, so they had lots of extra love to give to Bueller. And they grew their family even more when they adopted another bulldog named Kobe.

Kobe is deaf, so he follows his big brother, Bueller, around like a shadow. They do everything together! They love to take walks and play at the beach or the dog park.

And Bueller and Kobe are always up for a relaxing wagon ride, too!

When Bueller was a puppy, it was hard to believe that one day he would be such a strong—and fast!—bulldog. He's so happy he got a second chance and found his forever family.

walked straight to her home office to set Giselle down. Holly looked at the small ball of fluff lying next to her. She hoped Giselle's breathing would slow down now that they were at home.

Oh my gosh, what did I do? Holly thought. She had brought so many cats into her home before without a problem or a worry. But this cat was different. She was unlike any other cat Holly had cared for.

"There's no manual for taking home your first potato cat," she said to herself.

Since the beginning, Holly and her best friend had been referring to this little cat as a "potato cat" because she was the same size and shape as a potato. That's exactly what Giselle looked like to Holly—a snuggly potato. Holly had planned on changing Giselle's name, and Potato seemed like the perfect fit.

"You *are* a potato," she told the cat. It was decided. Giselle, formerly known as Munchkin, would now be called Potato.

Potato was finally sitting still on a soft surface. She had been picked up and moved around a lot over the past thirty minutes. Now she was just happy to be sitting so she could catch her breath and try to figure out where she was. Someone nice was talking to her. She recognized the voice. She started sniffing around so she could understand more about this new place. There had been a lot of change in Potato's life over the past few weeks. And she had met a lot of people. It was overwhelming. She hoped this place was one where she could stay for a while. She liked that it was quiet. It helped her calm down.

Potato was very affectionate. She started to settle down in her new home within hours. It was only the first night, but she seemed to know she was safe here and that her life was going to get better. Holly set down Potato on a soft bed in the home office, which she had transformed into a special bedroom for the new cat. It had soft, cushy blankets and bedding on the ground, and a camera so Holly could keep an eye on Potato when she went to work. The first thing Potato did was sniff out the litter box and pee.

"Yay! You know what that is already," Holly said. She lay down on the floor near the little cat. She knew that holding Potato was a no-no, so she figured she'd be doing a lot of lying on the ground as she got used to her new friend.

"I just want to make you comfortable," Holly explained. She kept talking out loud. She hoped to voice train Potato, which meant that Potato would understand certain words. Those words could help her get used to her environment and warn her if Holly had to pick her up or do something else unexpected.

Holly had closed the French doors to the office, but peeking through the windows on the other side were two of her other cats, Lady and Olive. Olive sniffed along the bottom edge of the door. Holly's cats were used to seeing foster cats in their home for short periods of time. But Olive reacted differently to Potato. Usually she would just glare at new pets—and humans—until they got scared and left the room. But she seemed to know that Potato was different and that she was sick. It was like she knew she wasn't a foster cat and was welcoming her to the family.

So far, everything was going as planned. Holly was smitten with Potato. She knew that together they could get through any obstacle that was thrown their way.

* * *

Less than twenty-four hours later, Potato was back in the hospital. And by the end of the week, she was in the hospital again. For the next two months, midnight emergency room visits were a regular part of Potato's life. Holly had taken care of sick animals since she was a kid. But this cat needed *a lot* of help.

Despite the hospital visits, though, Potato was doing really well. Holly was amazed on a daily basis by this little cat's good spirits. She had been born with a lot of issues, but she didn't care. She was always in a good mood. Potato was a joyful, playful cat—and her fur was growing in so nicely!

Holly liked to tap her fingers around on the floor and Potato would chase them.

"You're such a happy little sweet potato," Holly said to the cat as she texted Alyssa. She was sending photos so Alyssa could post them for Potato's followers. Here was Potato getting to know her new cat siblings. Potato resting in a sunbeam streaming through the window in Holly's living room. Potato wearing a little pair of cat-sized reindeer antlers. Her followers loved seeing these updates. But the reality was that they had no idea how sick she was.

Potato was getting used to her new home. There seemed to be at least four other furry individuals living with her. And the nice lady sure did talk a lot. She also gave her wet food that was so delicious. Sometimes when Potato was feeling sick, she had to be taken to a lot of different places. It made her dizzy. But she'd always eventually make it back home with all four paws safely on the ground. She liked this place. She hoped she didn't have to leave again.

* * *

Holly had adopted Potato in November, and it was February now. She was at the vet's office for yet another visit. There was now a whole team of doctors who were working with Potato to try to find the best solution for her. Their goal was to give her the best quality of life. After studying Potato's X-rays, the vet team had finally figured out what might be causing her problems going to the bathroom. Her organs had always been too big for her tiny body, and her colon (the organ that helped her poop) was the same way. If they could perform a surgery to remove 70 percent of her colon, then Potato would be able to use her litter box without a problem.

The surgery was dangerous. However, it was Potato's only chance at avoiding pain and doctor's visits every few days. Holly didn't know what to do. It was her job to give Potato the best life possible.

I want her to know that I tried, Holly thought. She decided to move forward with the surgery. She scheduled it for the following week.

Holly called Alyssa, who had been posting weekly updates on Potato and photos of cats who needed to be adopted, just like she and Holly had planned. Holly knew that they had to update Potato's followers with the truth: Potato needed a major surgery, and they weren't sure how it would go. Holly had all the confidence in the world that the doctors would take care of Potato as best they could. However, a big surgery was always risky. So she had made a decision that surprised even herself.

"The Instagram page is getting to be too much for you," Holly said to Alyssa. "The followers will want more updates after the surgery, and just in case anything bad happens, I want her followers to hear it from me."

Holly was the one who had made the decision for Potato to get surgery. So she felt like it was her responsibility to share the news—and whatever happened afterward—with Potato's followers. Alyssa understood. It was decided: Holly was taking over Potato's social media. Holly shared an update immediately.

"Hey, everyone! Potato's mom here! I wanted to personally give you an update about how she's been doing because I know how much you all love her. She has been doing so good, but she has been dealing with one major issue. She's been officially scheduled for surgery next week, and it should fix the ongoing problem. She is such a strong and resilient girl. Please keep her in your thoughts and send all the positive vibes her way. She's the happiest little pepita! Thank you all for your ongoing well wishes for her, and I'll keep you updated as she recovers. All the love from Potato and her fuzzy siblings."

Potato's followers were excited to hear a message directly from Holly.

"Sending love! She's so lucky to have you!"

"It makes me weep to see this little potato so loved."

"Thanks for taking such great care of her."

"I hope the surgery goes well and helps the problem."

"Please give her a kiss and a belly rub for me."

As she thought about the surgery, Holly was nervous—just like any cat mom would be. But by this time next week, she hoped she would have a good update to share with her followers.

CHAPTER 6

RECOVERY

POTATO'S SURGERY WAS DONE. IT had been a long, stressful day, but it went as well as it could have. Potato had had to stay in the hospital for four days, and Holly visited her every night. But now Holly was finally allowed to bring her home. She had blocked off her entire weekend so she could care for the little cat around the clock.

She placed Potato in the home office to rest. Olive was the only cat to come in and check on her. She sniffed Potato. Olive was usually so sassy and could come across as mean, so it was special to see her act so nurturing toward Potato. Olive could tell Potato needed time to recover before she'd go back to her usual playful self. Potato would need a week of antibiotics, some pain medicine, and lots of rest.

But within a few days, Potato was like a whole new cat!

Holly posted an update for Potato's followers: "So happy to be home! I can't thank the people at the MSPCA enough for everything they did for Potato, and the nurses and doctors for helping me fight for her life! The surgery was her only shot at any quality of life, and I'm amazed daily with her now, surviving and thriving. She truly is a special being, and even with how bad she felt back then, you could see how much she is just a happy little potato cat!"

Holly was so grateful for everyone's support, and so relieved to be sharing a happy update. Especially since she had gotten some bad news about Olive recently. But she didn't want to think about that right now. Potato deserved a little celebration.

"It's like night and day!" she said to her tiny cat. Potato was clearly feeling much better now—she was so happy, playful, and hungry! "You would eat all the food in the world if I'd let you," she added as she gave her some wet cat food as a snack after her medicine.

Most importantly, Potato could now go to the bathroom without a problem. No more midnight emergency room visits! Potato was doing so well that Holly opened the office doors so the little cat had free range all the way to the couch in the living room. (Holly had added a baby gate to keep her from wandering too far.) Potato's little world was already getting bigger.

Holly always kept the floor clear in the office and in the living room so that Potato could explore without running into anything. One time, she had walked beneath a plant stand and couldn't figure out how to get back out, so Holly blocked off that path. This cat was so small that she could walk under things no other cat could fit under. One day she hoped that Potato would be able to roam the whole house without help, but she'd have to learn it very slowly, one room at a time. It would probably take a year—or more.

Potato felt amazing. She was back home, and it was like everything had changed over the past few days. She just felt better. Happier. And even more ready to play and explore! She had twice as much room to run around now. And Olive was being so nice to her. But Potato was worried about Olive. She didn't seem like herself lately. Maybe something was wrong. Potato would pay extra attention to her. But right now, she wanted to go explore the living room one more time. She liked to walk around the edges of the room over and over again. She almost had it memorized. Once she had a room memorized, she could get around without bumping into anything. And then she could find that cool scratching toy again.

"Oh my god, you're playing!" Holly said.

It was the first time she had seen Potato really play with a toy. The scratching toy had a built-in ball track that was easy for Potato to push. Holly gave her some more toys that crinkled. She figured that toys that made noise would be easier for a blind cat to play with. She was so proud of Potato.

It had been two weeks since Potato's surgery, and she was doing great. But now there was another cat lying in Potato's office bed. It was Olive, who had just returned home from her own surgery. Last month, Holly had felt a lump while she was petting Olive. The vet had removed a large tumor, and now Olive had a row of stitches on her side. Potato came up and sniffed the black cat. Olive looked so tired, and a little uncomfortable. She was wearing a cone around her head so that she wouldn't lick her stitches. Holly could see Olive calm down once Potato was nearby.

Holly pet Olive softly. Olive was sick, but it was so sweet to see Potato being the strong one and comforting her, just like Olive had comforted Potato when she first joined their family. Lady, Holly's orange-and-black calico cat, was avoiding Olive, even though they were usually very close. So it meant even more—to both Holly and Olive—that Potato was being so friendly.

When Holly adopted Potato, she knew that the Munchkin cat was sick and might not live long. But she never expected that Potato would become such a strong and healthy cat while one of her healthy cats grew so sick. Over the next few weeks, Holly remained concerned about Olive. But there was a bright spot during this time: Potato kept growing stronger. She was the little cat that could!

Potato had even started to get comfortable sitting on Holly's lap, which was a big deal.

Holly started a tradition on Saturdays called "Caturday Night Couch Cuddles." She made a nest of blankets on the couch and let Potato know that she was safe somewhere besides the ground—in this case, the couch. Each week, Potato got less stressed out about being lifted up. Now Holly would say, "Do you want to do lap cuddles?" And Potato would get into position near Holly's feet and lift her head, which meant she was ready to be picked up. Sometimes she'd even climb off Holly's lap and explore the couch a bit. Holly hoped that eventually they could do this every day.

Potato understood other voice cues, too: "Do you want to clean your face?"; "Do you want to do medicine?"; and "Do you want to get in your nest?" Potato's "nest" was her bed next to the couch. This was one smart kitty! She was also starting to learn all of her nicknames besides

Potato, like "Sweet Potato," "Bitty Girl," and "Pepita."

Olive got up from the bed, and Holly watched her move across the office slowly. Potato seemed to watch, too, as her friend left the room.

Potato wanted to play, but she needed to check on Olive first. These days, Potato could explore the office, the living room, the kitchen, and the bathroom. She sniffed around and found Olive resting on the soft bath mat. She lay down next to her. Potato had felt amazing after her surgery, but she could tell Olive still wasn't feeling that great after hers. Potato hoped that a few cuddles would make Olive feel better.

Holly was grateful that Potato was being a good friend to Olive. Right now, they just had to keep Olive comfortable. It was so sweet to see Potato helping. Whenever Olive lay on the floor, Potato would find and lie next to her. Holly wasn't surprised to see the two of them cuddling in the bathroom.

Holly turned on the faucet. It was time for Potato to have her daily bath. Potato knew the sound of a bath meant that it was time for her to be cleaned. She didn't love bath time, but she went along with it. Afterward, Holly let Potato rest by the fireplace, where she would lick her paws. Olive joined her.

The thing I love about rescue cats is that you usually have to earn their trust and love, Holly thought as she looked at Olive and Potato lying side by side. It was so rewarding when she took an animal into her home—one who was usually scared and confused about what was happening—and showed them understanding and patience. She loved showing these cats that it was okay to trust and love again. And when they snuggled her, it was the absolute best.

That's why she continued to rescue cats like Olive and Potato. They took a lot of work, and sometimes the road was filled with bumps. She never quite knew how the journey would end. But she loved being along for the ride.

CHAPTER 7

FRIENDS

DON'T EVEN THINK OF CROSSING MY path! Potato loved to guard the water bowls. She knew that the other cats liked to drink water, so hanging out over there was the easiest way for her to find a friend to play with. She stayed very still and imagined that they didn't know she was there. But no matter how slowly they sneaked by, she'd hear them. No one could outsmart her. Wait, what was that? Jack was coming. Pounce!

"Miss Sassy Spud!" Holly said. "Be careful chasing around your brother!"

Potato was playing her usual game with Jack, Holly's male orange tabby cat. Over the past few months, Potato had been recovering so well from her surgery that Holly had let her explore even more of the house. Most recently, she had mastered the kitchen. She'd stand on the kitchen mat (so she knew where she was) and then wait for Jack to try to tiptoe slowly toward his water bowl, which was at the other end of the room. As soon as he got near, Potato would jump out and surprise him. Whenever she ran around the kitchen to chase him, she'd come back to her mat so she could "reset" and know where she was.

Deep down she is just a normal, playful kitty, Holly thought. *And so is Jack.* She loved seeing the bond between the two of them grow. Watching them chase each other around was the funniest thing ever. Even though Potato couldn't see Jack, she could hear him. No matter how quietly he tried to sneak by to get a sip of water, she was ready to attack him like a little troll guarding a bridge. They'd play for about twenty minutes, until Jack noticed that Potato's breathing was getting heavy and she needed a little break. Jack knew that Potato was different and that he had to be careful around her.

Holly was impressed with how gentle Jack was with Potato, but she was also impressed that Potato had memorized the layout of yet another room. There were a couple spots around their home, like the kitchen mat, that Potato used as a marker to help her understand where she was.

Now she rarely bumped into things even when she was running. It was unbelievable!

Lady watched from the sidelines as usual. She was very protective of Potato and wanted to make sure Jack didn't accidentally hurt her. But Holly could tell that Lady was also jealous. She wanted to play, too! Holly pet Olive softly while she watched the other cats play. Olive wasn't playing with Jack or Potato, and she didn't seem interested in joining them. Throughout the whole summer, it seemed like Holly's friends kept saying to her: "I don't understand how Olive is so sick and Potato is doing so much better." She didn't understand, either.

Potato's ears perked up and her eyes turned toward the door.

"She definitely recognizes your voice!" Holly

said. It had been about six months since Potato's surgery, and they were back at the MSPCA for a routine checkup. Alyssa had just walked in to say hello. It was a hot August day in Boston, and Dr. Moses had a smile on her face while she was examining Potato. So far, everything looked great. The surgery had really helped! Holly was so relieved to hear this news. She could tell that her little potato kitty was living a great life, but it was always nice to hear the doctor confirm it.

Unfortunately, Olive's most recent appointment hadn't gone as well. She was getting very sick. Holly thought back to the first time she met Olive. She was a little six-week-old feral kitten who had been alone and in distress. She needed a home and Holly was happy to give her one. The first time Olive met anyone she tried to scare them. She'd hiss at you, especially if you looked like you were frightened. But if you laughed at her, she'd quickly become your best friend. Even though she was intimidating, she loved to wear costumes on Halloween, Easter, and Christmas. And she had formed such a sweet bond with Potato, which was the most unexpected thing of all. And now that Olive was going through her own rough time, Olive's friendship with Potato had become even more important. Holly was so thankful the two cats had each other.

A few weeks passed, and the summer weather had a hint of a cool autumn breeze in Boston. That morning, Holly found herself sitting on the bed. Tears were streaming down her face. Her poor Olive had just passed away. But right at her feet was her little potato kitty. Just before Olive had passed, Potato had walked in the room. *Animals just know,* Holly thought. *They know way better than we do.* Lady, Little Sister, and Jack, however, were staying far away. They sensed something was wrong; it was like they thought it was more respectful to leave Olive alone. But Potato was here for her friend. She had purposely walked into this room. It was really nice to see that she understood. She would be there for Holly now just like she was for Olive. Holly gave her kisses and whispered, "Thank you."

CHAPTER 8

COMPLETE

IT WAS A COOL OCTOBER MORNING.
Exactly one year since Munchkin-Giselle-
Potato-Pepita-Bitty Kitty Girl had been rescued.
The little family was eating breakfast, and Holly
hadn't turned away for more than a second, but
Potato had already stolen food from her brother
Jack's plate. She had quite the appetite! If Holly
wasn't looking, she'd eat all of Jack's and Lady's

food—if they'd let her. She might be blind, but she had great senses of hearing and smell. Her followers constantly asked, "How blind is she?" because she seemed like she could see—at least a little bit. Holly had to remind them all the time, "She is completely blind! But she's not held back by her conditions. She's just a happy potato!" It was just one more way this cat made her laugh.

After breakfast, Holly continued on with their morning routine. Potato now let Holly pick her up for lap cuddles and grooming every morning before she left for work. As soon as Holly sat down on the couch to slip into her shoes, Potato walked over. She knew that meant Holly was getting ready to leave for work—but not before giving Potato some cuddles first! Potato would stand near Holly's feet, then turn her body into position. Then Holly picked her up, brushed her, and pet her softly until she fell asleep for her morning nap. Holly would sit with her as long as she could, then would place her in her nest of blankets so she could nap peacefully. It was obviously a comforting routine for Potato, but it was equally comforting for Holly. She could find a moment of calm before she had to leave for work. It was the best way to start the day!

But today was an anniversary. An anniversary that had changed her life! Before she left for work, Holly had to share a special post with their followers to celebrate.

"One year ago today, a tiny cat named Munchkin was surrendered to the MSPCA. She was scared and in need of a lot of help. But she was given a chance, a new name, and had some amazing humans watching out for her. She's a little survivor and deserved the best care she could get. She's the little Potato that could. I thank you all for your love and support of this special spud over the last year."

Potato's followers couldn't believe a year had already passed. This little cat had come so far since then. Just twelve months before, she had been very sick, with matted hair and a lot of medical issues. Now she was a bundle of energy with a group of furry friends who loved to play with her, a loving mom, and a safe home. The supportive comments poured in:

"She's so precious!"

"I just love her!"

"Obviously, Potato hit the jackpot. You are an amazing cat mom!"

"Love her to the moon and back!"

Holly took down the last baby gate and opened up the last door. It had taken a year, but Potato was about to officially conquer the entire house. This blind cat could find her way around every room—except this last one. The final room was one Holly reserved especially for foster cats. Inside were a few cat beds, a scratching post, a litter box, and a rug of fake grass. Jack followed Potato inside.

Potato felt freedom! She could now walk around the entire house on her own. No more gates or doors to bump into. This last room was a challenge—she slowly walked on a floor that felt kind of weird and squishy, but Jack was nearby so she knew she was safe. He wanted to show her where all the best sleeping spots were. Exploring her home had been the most fun she'd ever had. She felt more confident, especially now that she could go to all the same places Jack and Lady did. She was so lucky to have a nice mom and nice cat friends. The past year had been the best.

Holly admired Potato as the little cat studied the final room of the house carefully and committed it to her memory. It had been a long and bumpy road for this tiny potato cat, but she had turned out to be a little warrior. Holly couldn't wait to let her followers know about Potato's big achievement. She laughed a little. If you had told her a year ago that she'd be sending daily updates to more than two hundred thousand online followers about the antics of her blind, three-pound cat, she would have thought you were crazy. She had even given Potato's followers a nickname: the Spud Squad.

Every day, Potato inspired Holly. Somehow,

this cat was the happiest pet she knew. Every day was brighter with Potato in it. "We all need more Potato in our lives," Holly said as she gave the little cat a belly rub. And that's exactly why she continued to share updates with her followers. It was a small act on Holly's part, but if even just one post helped a person or an animal who really needed it, it was worth it. She hoped each video and photo she shared would brighten someone else's day or encourage them to adopt a pet who might need a little extra care. After all, that's what it was all about. Taking care of one another.

THE MSPCA-ANGELL

Potato was rescued by the Massachusetts Society for the Prevention of Cruelty to Animals–Angell Animal Medical Center in Boston. The MSPCA–Angell (or MSPCA for short) was founded shortly after the Civil War in 1868, making it one of the first humane organizations in the United States. Humane societies work to end suffering in animals. The MSPCA's founder, George Thorndike Angell, was a lawyer in Boston who wanted to prevent cruelty to horses and other animals.

Today, the MSPCA rescues, shelters, protects, heals, and advocates for thousands of horses, farm animals, and companion animals like cats and dogs every year. With adoption centers and veterinary facilities throughout Massachusetts, its mission is to spread compassion and kindness toward animals.

BLIND PETS

Blindness might seem like a major setback for a pet, but animals like Potato prove that's not true! Blind or vision-impaired cats and dogs can live full, happy lives. Some pets are born blind, while others lose their vision as they get older. Either way, these animals have to be cared for in a special way. Here are some tips for living with a blind or vision-impaired pet:

START SLOW

Holly kept Potato in just one room in her house in order to keep her safe and prevent her from feeling overwhelmed. She slowly let her learn the other rooms one space at a time. Blind pets will do better if floors are free from clutter and if dangerous spots like stairs are blocked off with a baby gate. Holly also avoids moving her furniture around or making other big changes to how each room is arranged so Potato doesn't get confused.

SPEAK UP

Blind pets have to use their other senses in order to survive. Give them audio cues, like Holly does, before you touch them, pick them up, give them a bath, or do anything else that could startle them. Use the same cue every time so the pet can learn what it means.

USE MARKERS

Blind pets will also use their sense of touch and sense of smell to navigate a home. Just like Holly's kitchen mat became very important for Potato, a rug in front of a litter box or food bowl can help your pet find what he or she needs. But remember, if you remove that rug, it could be very confusing for a blind pet! Don't move familiar items unless you have to.

STICK TO A ROUTINE

All pets can memorize and become familiar with a daily routine, and it's especially important for blind pets so they know what to expect in their day. This schedule, combined with cues from their other senses (like sense of touch, smell, and hearing), can ensure their days are filled with fun instead of stress.

KEEP THEM MOVING

Toys and games can keep your animal active— both physically and mentally. All cats and dogs love to play, even if they can't see! Try puzzle toys, sound-making toys, and scent-tracking games to help them gain confidence. Walks around the block with a leash are possible, too, if your pet is trained to use one.

BEWARE OF CHANGE

New people, new places, and new things can be extra stressful for a blind pet. Pets will need time to adjust to any changes in their environment. A stranger entering your home could cause alarm. So a blind pet might do better waiting it out in another room until the person leaves. Blind pets need small adjustments and extra thought, but it's worth the effort to keep them happy and safe!

BUELLER'S STORY

BUELLER

CHAPTER 1

A SECOND CHANCE

DR. LAURIE BUZZED THROUGH THE
hallways of the Sacramento Society for the
Prevention of Cruelty to Animals, or the SSPCA.
Her red stethoscope hung from her neck and she
carried a folder in her hand. It was another busy
day on a sunny January afternoon, but she loved
her job as a veterinarian. As chief of Shelter
Medicine, every day was different. There were

two hundred to three hundred animals at the SSPCA who needed exams, treatments, and sometimes special surgeries. But regardless of what each day held, it was spent pursuing the same cause: making sure the pets here lived the happiest lives they could. That was the same mission that guided more than one hundred other employees and volunteers at the shelter as well.

This afternoon, her attention was being called to a special patient: an eight-week-old bulldog who had just been surrendered by a dog breeder. The puppy had already been given a general physical exam by an animal care technician, but something was wrong. That's why Dr. Laurie was here. As she walked into the office, she could see her coworkers Sarah and Jaime cuddling a bulldog puppy and staring into his sweet brown eyes. Jaime was responsible for keeping track of the animals when they first came into the shelter, and Sarah helped those animals eventually get adopted.

"Even though he's two months old, he can't walk at all," Sarah told Dr. Laurie. Puppies are usually walking and standing by the time they're three weeks old. Obviously, something wasn't right. Some animals who arrived at the shelter simply needed to be treated for fleas before they could be adopted. But it wouldn't be that simple for this puppy. Sarah knew he'd have a much harder time getting adopted if he couldn't walk. It broke her heart.

"We think it's swimmer syndrome," Jaime added.

Dr. Laurie took the pup from Sarah's arms. He had been cuddling up in her blonde hair. Dr. Laurie held him to her chest as she pet him softly, letting him rest against the maroon scrubs she was wearing. Then she carefully set the pup back down. His ears were perky and his eyes were curious. But his chest was flat and his four limbs splayed out to the side so he was unable to stand or walk. She had no doubt about what was wrong.

"You're right. It is swimmer syndrome," she confirmed. "His muscles are too weak to pull his legs in toward the middle, so they just splay outward."

Dr. Laurie had helped kittens with swimmer syndrome at the shelter before, but never a puppy. Usually, a pet with this condition would start treatment at three or four weeks old. This bulldog was far past that age, and to make things worse, there was also something unusual about his right leg. It almost looked like it had been broken but then healed the wrong way. A surgery might be the only way to fix that. At about ten pounds, the little guy just couldn't hold his body up. It would definitely take longer than normal for him to recover.

The SSPCA was known for rescuing animals in need, healing them, and then adopting them out to the perfect forever home. They helped up to five thousand animals every year. Dr. Laurie had seen everything from bad skin diseases and broken legs to injured eyes and lost teeth. Although she'd taken on tough cases before, this one made her nervous. This pup would need a lot of special care and rehabilitation before he would be able to walk. The first step would be finding him a foster home, which was a family who would care for him while he was being treated, until he was ready to find a forever home. It had to be someone who understood his situation and was willing to work with him every day until he recovered.

Jaime tucked her dark brown hair behind her

ears and observed the puppy splayed out on the counter. "Wow, that does look bad," she said as she realized how helpless this little pup was. His legs couldn't support his body at all. From the moment she saw this puppy, Jaime knew she needed to help him. *Sometimes you see an animal, and you just feel the connection*, she thought. Could she be the one to foster him? But taking in a foster pet was a lot of work. Jaime and the little pup gazed lovingly into each other's brown eyes.

"He has soulful eyes and just wants to be loved," Jaime said.

Sarah's blue eyes grew big. Was Jaime considering fostering the puppy?

"I'm done for. He's coming home with me tonight." Jaime scooped the bulldog into her arms.

Sarah and Dr. Laurie cheered. They knew Jaime and her husband, Joe, would make great foster parents. Jaime was a dog lover, and it would be easy for her to bring the pup in to work every day for checkups. He could sit and play next to her desk during the day. And they'd be able to watch this puppy gain strength and make progress every day at the shelter. At least that's what they hoped would happen.

The three women looked at the little puppy again. They could tell that he wanted to live. His body may have been limp, but his eyes were bright and full of energy. It was something they saw often in the animals who were brought into the shelter. Dr. Laurie liked to call it *joie de vivre*, which is French for "joy of living." It made her job easier. If a pet had a will to live, then she would do everything she could to try to help him recover. That will to live often rubbed off on her and gave her the energy she needed to keep working hard even when things got tough.

"So we agree," Dr. Laurie said to her co-workers as she adjusted her glasses and flashed a smile. "The goal is to get this pup standing on all four paws as soon as possible. It might be a lot of work, but let's give it a try."

"Okay, Bueller," Jaime said, naming him after the lead character in a popular movie from the 1980s. "You're coming home with me."

Jaime pulled the baby bassinet out of her closet. Her husband, Joe, had bought it when they'd adopted their own rescue dog, a boxer named Ozzy. She had thought Joe was crazy when he brought home a human baby bassinet for a dog, but the bassinet ended up working really well for Ozzy. She knew it would be perfect for Bueller, too. He wouldn't be able to get out, and it could be carried easily from the living room to the bedroom. It would be really convenient in the middle of the night when he whimpered. Jaime would just be able to reach over and pet him.

"I can comfort you without leaving my nice, cozy bed," Jaime explained to the bulldog. This little guy needed constant care. Since he couldn't stand, he had to be cleaned as soon as he went to the bathroom. If he didn't have a clean, dry bed and clean, dry skin, his belly would get a rash. Keeping him nearby would be especially important.

She set Bueller into the bassinet by the stone fireplace. A cozy fire was warming up her living room. Ozzy jumped onto the soft brown chair that matched his fur color and peeked inside the white bassinet. The little bulldog puppy had nuzzled into a tan blanket. Ozzy loved when Jaime brought home foster dogs.

"You'll be a great foster brother," Jaime said as she gave Ozzy a belly rub.

Bueller wasn't quite sure what was going on. Today had been very exciting. He was brought to a new place and a lot of smiling faces had looked down on him. Everyone seemed to love him very much. They had wrapped his leg, which made him feel better. They had given him a lot of kisses and scratches, too. There was a big dog looking at him right now, much bigger than his brothers and sisters had been. But he seemed nice. So did the nice lady who was petting him. After traveling in a box, and a car, and now something called a bassinet, he was exhausted. The bassinet was oh-so-soft. And he was oh-so-sleepy.

CHAPTER 2

TIME FOR A SWIM

THE SSPCA HAD A BIG FOLLOWING ON social media. Their followers loved to see which pets they were currently treating. Sarah knew they had to introduce this swimmer syndrome pup to the world. Donations from followers and well wishes would help this little bulldog get through his long recovery. He needed all the love and help he could get.

"Meet Bueller," the post said. "Our veterinary team is putting their heads together to develop a treatment plan. Stay tuned for updates and please send good thoughts his way!"

Over one hundred people commented.

"Sending prayers for this sweet baby!"

"So happy you're working with him. I've seen miracles happen with your staff!"

"Aww, what a cutie! Hope you can find a solution."

Others offered advice like trying splints, taping his legs closer together, or slings that could help him walk. Sarah knew that Dr. Laurie would come up with the best solution for this particular pup. Every dog was different, and so was every recovery. Dr. Laurie had already done research to try to find the perfect plan for Bueller. There were a lot of options to consider. But there was one treatment that she knew would help for sure: water therapy. Funny enough, swimming was one of the best treatments for swimmer syndrome. Being in a pool would allow Bueller's legs to move in a more natural position underneath his body because he wouldn't have to hold his weight up. This could help him build up his muscles without putting strain on his limbs.

Jaime brought Bueller in to work for his first day of recovery. *This is our new routine,* she thought as she carried Bueller through the front doors. Instead of heading toward her office, she brought Bueller to a special room where a metal tub and an orange life jacket awaited him. The first step in Bueller's path to recovery was about to begin. But how would he react?

Ooh, the water was nice. Bueller had been lowered into a little metal tub with warm water. His natural reaction was to start moving his front and back paws. He had never really been able to do that before. He had seen his brothers and sisters walk around, but whenever he'd tried to move his legs, nothing much happened. But now here he was in a new place in a warm tub with one of the nice ladies cheering him on. She told him he was swimming. And she said, "There you go, Bueller!" He had never been swimming before. This was . . . interesting.

Bueller moved slowly, but then he moved faster. Whew! This was a little tiring. Now he was making the water splash—cool! Splash, splash, splash! Phew! Now he was even more tired. He was done now, but he couldn't get his legs to stop moving. Thankfully, the nice lady lifted him out of the tub. He needed a rest.

Dr. Laurie prescribed a ten-minute water therapy session every day. Jaime knew that swimming was good for toning Bueller's muscles, but he was exhausted afterward. When the swim vest came out, Bueller knew what was coming. Water equals work. And when he got tired of exercising, he would huff or let out a long dramatic sigh.

"Quite the drama king!" Sarah said to Jaime. It had been just four days since Bueller had been dropped off at the shelter, but it seemed like he was already gaining some strength thanks to his therapy sessions. Sarah wanted to be optimistic that Bueller would fully recover, but it was too soon to tell. Jaime and Dr. Laurie were doing an amazing job caring for Bueller, but bulldogs are shaped differently than other dogs. They have short legs that keep their wide bodies low to the ground. So although water therapy had worked well for other dog breeds, it didn't mean it would work perfectly for Bueller. Plus, Bueller was already growing quickly. They wouldn't be able to hold him in the tub of water for long.

Still, they were keen to share an update with their followers about Bueller's progress. They posted a video of his latest water therapy session. The caption said, "One of the best treatments for swimmer syndrome is . . . swimming! We are also working on a series of splints and a puppy 'baby bouncer' to help Bueller learn to walk." Then they shared a link for anyone who was willing to donate money toward Bueller's recovery. The donations started pouring in from social media followers.

"I was so heartbroken seeing this puppy, but now I'm elated. Keep us updated!"

"He's just so flippin' cute!"

"I had to share this. He's one tough puppy!"

"Keep on swimming, Bueller!"

Everyone at the SSPCA knew that Bueller was cute. And his swimming sessions were especially adorable. Bueller hadn't even been there a week, and he was already getting some major attention online. The Dodo, a digital media company that tells stories about animals, wrote about Bueller's story. Then a local news channel stopped by. More and more people were falling in love with Bueller and following his journey to recovery. This was the first time the shelter had had a social media star within their midst! The comments kept pouring in:

"Please keep us posted on Bueller and let us know how we can help!"

"Don't give up on him. He's going to be okay!"

"He's so sweet!"

But as his foster mom, Jaime just wanted to focus on Bueller's recovery. The swimming videos were cute, but they had to keep their ultimate goal in mind: getting Bueller standing on all four legs. Once he could stand and had made some progress toward walking, there was a much better chance that Sarah, who was in charge of adoptions at the shelter, could find him a forever family.

When Jaime first brought Bueller home, Dr. Laurie had given her splints to help keep his joints straight. They didn't help. Next they tried braces and other supports, as well as taping his legs into a more normal position. But each idea ended up failing, so then they'd have to try something new. At home, Jaime made sure to always position Bueller's legs directly underneath his body when she held him. It was her way of "training" his joints.

All these attempts to get Bueller to walk were tough on everyone. It was a roller coaster of emotions! It was hard to get over a failure when Jaime knew everyone was counting on her to get this dog walking. But Bueller was never in pain, and he was always in such a happy mood. The physical therapy exercises Jaime was doing with him would help strengthen the puppy's muscles so he could eventually hold his weight up, and maybe even walk on his own. That was still the plan. Hopefully it would work.

It had been ten days since Bueller's first water therapy session. He and Jaime were back at the SSPCA. Jaime watched Bueller as he lay on a gray blanket next to her desk. He was playing with a red ball and a gray stuffed dog toy that squeaked. As he attacked the toy and shook it in his mouth, he lifted his butt in the air. His back legs were supporting his body! It was just for a few seconds, but it was huge news. She called in Dr. Laurie.

"This is a big milestone!" Dr. Laurie said. "Here's the first step toward success." She scratched the little pup's belly and told him, "You have this determination to get what you want."

Jaime agreed. Things were looking up. Maybe Bueller would be walking before she knew it.

CHAPTER 3

BABY STEPS

JUST TWO DAYS LATER, JAIME'S
husband, Joe, was putting the finishing touches
on another idea that might help Bueller walk.
Now that the puppy was starting to put weight
on his legs, Joe wanted to make him a little
cart that could help him move forward. That
made Jaime smile. Joe looked like he was having
so much fun. When Jaime had first met Joe, he

didn't even like having pet hair on his clothes. Now they shared their home with five dogs, three cats, thirteen chickens, sixteen ducks, two geese, and seven pygmy goats. Joe had definitely come around! They fostered animals all the time, too. Joe knew these pets needed extra time and love. Making a cart for Bueller was his way of showing that he understood.

Jaime couldn't wait to see Bueller try out his cart. It had four wheels and was made out of PVC pipe, swivel wheels, bungee cords, and a fleece blanket with leg holes cut into it. It allowed Bueller to stand inside with his stomach supported by the blanket while his feet lightly touched the ground. In theory, every time Bueller stepped, the device could wheel forward. Jaime placed it on her carpeted living room floor and then placed Bueller into the sling, with one foot in each of the four holes.

The sling held most of his body weight perfectly, and the holes that were cut into the blanket helped him get used to having his legs in the correct position.

Jaime let go. Now Bueller was "standing" with his four legs directly beneath him. He looked excited. He was ready to go! But he just stood there. He didn't understand what to do next. Jaime pushed the cart forward a little. It didn't really help.

Jaime and Joe looked at each other, concerned. Then Joe had an idea. He set a bowl of kibble a few steps away from Bueller. As soon as the food came out, Bueller started putting pressure on one of his front legs.

"That's all the motivation he needs!" Jaime laughed. This dog loved food.

Bueller was eyeing the bowl of food in front of him. Mmm, kibble. But how to get to it? The nice lady had pushed him forward a little bit, but then she stopped. Why didn't she keep pushing him? The food was still far away. Bueller pressed down on one paw. He could feel the fluffy carpet below. He pushed down on the other paw. More fluffy carpet. But that kibble was still in the same place. The way Bueller saw it, there were two options: Someone could wheel him forward to the food, or someone could bring the food to him. He'd just stand here and wait till the humans figured it out.

Bueller practiced walking with the cart every day. And every day, he got a little more comfortable with it. He seemed to understand that when he stepped with one leg, the cart would move forward a little bit. But he didn't realize that the cart could help him walk wherever he wanted to go—including toward a bowl of food! Then one day it clicked. Bueller took a step. The cart wheeled forward. He took another step. The cart wheeled forward again. And then he kept going. He didn't stop this time. He was walking!

"It's like seeing your child take their first steps!" Jaime said to her husband. Joe watched eagerly next to her, proud of the contraption he had created and of the little pup for working so hard.

Bueller's body weight was still being supported by the fleece sling, but taking these steps was a huge milestone. Jaime could tell that Bueller was getting used to keeping his limbs directly under his body instead of spread out to the side. And his baby steps meant his muscles were getting stronger—a sign that hopefully one day soon he would be able to walk without any support. This homemade cart had worked! Everyone at the SSPCA couldn't believe Bueller's progress.

"It's your diligence and creativity that's making this work," Dr. Laurie told Jaime.

It was just what Jaime needed to hear. Tomorrow was the first day of February. Bueller had only been with Jaime for two weeks, and he was already taking steps. She knew there were lots of fans out there who were following along with Bueller's progress. She had to share this update with them. She knew they'd be just as proud of the puppy as she was. She posted a video of Bueller walking in her living room, and their followers went wild:

"Omg! Yes! He's getting so strong!"

"I'm getting tears in my eyes!"

"Nice moves, Bueller!"

"You are such a brave, inspirational puppy!"

The video was watched fifty-nine thousand times, and more than three thousand people liked it. It was amazing to see so many fans cheering on Bueller. Every small step was a reason to celebrate. Jaime was excited to see what the new month would bring. Maybe February would be the month that Bueller started to walk. Judging by his fast progress, it seemed possible. But it was also crazy to think how far he'd already come in such a short time.

As Jaime scrolled through the comments of her post, she noticed a different kind of message appearing more often:

"I would love to give this little man some love! Please let us know when he is available!"

"I have a feeling when Bueller is ready for adoption, there will be a mile-long line for him!"

"I will adopt him and work with him!"

As Bueller's popularity was growing, so were the number of people who wanted to adopt him. Jaime had always known that her time with Bueller was temporary. One day—maybe one day soon—he'd move on to his forever family. Would they love him as much as she loved him? No matter how many times Jaime fostered a pet, these thoughts ran through her head. It was always difficult to give up an animal who had become a part of your family—even if they'd only been with you for a short amount of time.

Sarah was impressed by all the attention Bueller was getting online. She knew now that his adoption would probably be different than most of the other animals she had worked with because of the number of social media fans he had. The shelter would have to be prepared for a lot of applications. But how would they decide who would be the perfect fit? They'd have to think of something special for this unique pup. Once in the past, they'd asked families to include an essay along with their application to adopt a special-needs pet. The pet required extra care, and the essay helped the team at the SSPCA understand whether the family who applied was emotionally ready to care for this pet. Perhaps they should do this for Bueller, too. But right now, they had to stay focused on what mattered the most: getting Bueller to walk on his own.

CHAPTER 4

BIG NEWS

IT HAD BEEN ONE WEEK SINCE Bueller first walked in his cart. It was a nice February weekend in Sacramento, and Jaime was at home alone with the dogs.

"We could all use some air and sunshine," she said to Bueller and Ozzy. She carried Bueller outside and Ozzy followed. She didn't grab Bueller's cart. Jaime had a feeling that

Bueller was ready. Or was it too soon? There was only one way to find out. She set the puppy on the grass. He wasn't sure what to do. He sniffed. Jaime took a few steps backward.

"Bueller," she called.

Bueller popped up. He was standing on all fours and it felt okay. He moved one leg forward, just like he had with the cart. Then another leg. Step. Step. Step. The nice lady was clapping and calling his name. Step, step, step! He was doing it! Freedom! Bueller ran through the dirt. He ran through the grass. He took a break. Then he ran some more. He sniffed Ozzy. He sniffed the nice lady. He took a break. He sniffed the grass over there. He took another break. And then he sniffed the grass over there. Then another break. This running thing was awesome. He could sniff everything! And the next time he saw a bowl of kibble, he could run to it. Yes!

It had finally happened: Bueller took his first steps. Jaime couldn't believe what she was seeing. He was running out of pure excitement. All of their hard work had paid off! The water therapy, the leg exercises, the puppy cart. All of it had helped. His leg muscles were finally strong enough to hold up his body weight. Bueller could walk. Heck, Bueller could run! Jaime grabbed her phone and hit record. She had to get a video and share it with everyone.

On Monday morning, Bueller's fans couldn't believe the post that appeared in their feeds: "Well, it happened this weekend . . . Bueller walked!!!"

"Go, Bueller, go!"

"I'm so happy! This is HUGE progress in such a short amount of time!"

"Congrats to Bueller and to the SSPCA staff for your dedication!"

"This is the best news for my Monday!"

"This made me cry! So sweet!"

The video got seventy-one thousand views, almost six thousand likes, and more than five hundred comments. Bueller was officially famous. The next day, The Dodo posted a video about Bueller's amazing progress, from lying down totally helpless to running through the grass in just a few weeks. Thousands and thousands of people watched their video and even more comments like this one came rolling in:

"I'd love to hug the little cutie. Will he be up for adoption?!"

Now that Bueller could walk, the SSPCA

couldn't ignore questions about his forever home anymore. He was ready for adoption. Dr. Laurie and the staff gathered to discuss it. Bueller's first steps were still fresh in all of their minds, and they were just about in tears thinking of the amazing things he had achieved since his arrival in January.

"That was pretty awesome," Dr. Laurie said as she rewatched the video of Bueller prancing happily through Jaime's backyard. "Because, you know, you're never quite sure if you're gonna get there."

She meant that it was never guaranteed that an animal was going to recover. But Bueller had. He had exceeded their expectations! The team nodded with tears in their eyes. Dr. Laurie was getting choked up, too. This was surprising to her, because she didn't cry easily. In her job, she had to deal with ups and downs every day. She had to stay tough and stay professional.

It allowed her to focus on the problem in front of her so she could solve it. But today was a day to celebrate.

"He is gonna have a good life," she added.

The team decided on a few things: Whoever adopted Bueller would need to be prepared for potentially expensive medical issues in the future. He had a slight limp when he walked, so his right leg most likely needed surgery. Also, as the foster parent, Jaime let them know that Bueller loved being the center of attention at her home. The adopter should be able to give him all of the love and care he needed to be the best dog he could be. And finally, whoever wanted to adopt him should include a letter describing why Bueller was the perfect fit for their family.

Ten days later, the news was out: Bueller was officially up for adoption.

CHAPTER 5

LOTS OF LOVE

LINDSEY WAS BRUSHING HER LONG blonde hair while getting ready for work. From the bathroom, she could hear the TV playing. *Good Day Sacramento*, her favorite local morning show, was on. When she heard the next feature, "I'm Cute, Adopt Me!" start, she poked her head out of the bathroom quickly. Lindsey had always been an animal lover. As a kid, she had dreamed of becoming a veterinarian one day. And for as long as she remembered, she had always had the urge to pet every dog she came across. She never became a veterinarian, but she and her now-husband did get their very own dog, who they loved very much: a white English bulldog named Chubbs. He had been the best dog—full of love and wrinkles. He had loved to skateboard and had been obsessed with his orange Frisbee. He could never get enough belly scratches or afternoon naps on the couch. They both missed him every day.

Lindsey started walking slowly toward the TV so she could see better. A picture of a tiny brown English bulldog puppy was staring back at her. *What a sweet boy,* she thought. His name was Bueller. Apparently, when he had been dropped off at the SSPCA, he couldn't even walk. He had something called swimmer syndrome. But now, after a lot of practice and a lot of love, the little pup was able to move around on his own. Lindsey watched lovingly as a video played of the puppy trotting across the floor. He struggled a bit, but it was easy to see he was a determined little guy who wouldn't let anything hold him back. Lindsey felt her heart melting. *Wait, did they say he's up for adoption?*

But she couldn't. Today was February 18. Less than two months ago, she and her husband, Alex, had lost Chubbs to cancer. Chubbs had been in their lives for nine years. He was even a part of their wedding! She glanced at her favorite photo from that day: She was wearing her white lace dress, and Alex was wearing his light gray suit. Chubbs sat faithfully between them wearing a black bow tie like a true gentleman. It looked like Alex had just told a joke because they were all laughing—even Chubbs.

The sun had been shining so beautifully on that October afternoon, and the day had been filled with friends and family. They had no idea that by the end of December their furry best friend would be gone.

After Chubbs passed away, the warm northern California weather had turned gloomy. It rained all of January. Their house was eerily silent. No more loud breathing from Chubbs or naptime snoring. No more nails clacking on the floor as he followed Lindsey and Alex around the house. No more millions of slobbery morning kisses for her and Alex. The quiet was deafening. But now that it was February, things seemed to be changing for the better. The rain had finally stopped. The warm California sun had returned. After lots of tears, she and Alex were just starting to accept the loss of their dear Chubbs. Really, it had only been a few days since things had started to seem brighter. How could she even consider adopting another dog already?

Lindsey shut off the TV, said good-bye to Alex, and left for work.

"Hey, will you cover the phone for me?" Lindsey asked her coworker. She was an assistant in a marketing department, and she was responsible for answering the phone as soon as it rang. But she couldn't get her mind off Bueller. The first thing she did when she sat down at her desk that morning was go to the *Good Day Sacramento* website and read more about the little bulldog. She read his story over and over again, but it was the last sentence that she was focused on: "If you are interested in adopting Bueller, submit an essay and an application to the Sacramento SPCA by February 25." That was just one week away. She had already emailed Bueller's article and video to Alex. She didn't have a grand plan in mind, but she had a strong feeling in her heart that she couldn't shake off. She picked up her phone and called her husband. Was she really doing this? Were they ready to adopt another dog?

"He's going to need extra love and support and care," Lindsey explained. "And he may need surgery, too."

Lindsey and Alex had experience setting money aside for a dog's health needs. Chubbs had needed many treatments while he attempted to fight off cancer. It was expensive, but every extra day they got to spend with him and help relieve his pain was worth it.

"I wasn't sure if we were ever gonna get another dog because of the feelings we had with

Chubbs on those final days," Alex said. Chubbs had passed away at home with Alex and Lindsey by his side. Even though it was a very sad day, they were so glad the three of them were able to be together in his final moments.

"But for the nine years before that, think of how much happiness he brought to our lives," Lindsey added.

"When Bueller looked into the camera, it was like he was looking at us," Alex said. Lindsey could hear the love growing in his voice. If he had watched the video as many times as she had, she knew it would be hard for him to say no.

"I want to be a part of Bueller's journey, and I want him to be a part of our family," Lindsey said. She held her breath. "Do you think we're ready?" There was silence on the other end.

"You know what? Let's do it."

Lindsey hadn't felt this happy in a long time.

She hung up her phone and dashed back to her computer. Even though it was still hard to think about Chubbs and write about his death, the essay flowed out of her within minutes. After all, Chubbs was an important part of their story, and it showed they were capable of giving all their love to a bulldog. She attached her favorite wedding day photo, the one where Chubbs was laughing, and sent off their application. She knew Alex would love the essay when she showed it to him later that night. Even if they never heard back, she was thankful to Bueller for bringing some light into their lives. He had already helped the two of them move on from some of their pain. Dogs were always good at that.

CHAPTER 6

A NEW FAMILY

WHEN THE SSPCA POSTED ABOUT Bueller's adoption, the applications quickly started flowing in. That same day, a video had aired on *Good Day Sacramento* sharing Bueller's story and the fact that he was ready to be loved by one lucky family. The team at the SSPCA could barely keep up with all the media requests about Bueller and the comments that were appearing on their social media feeds.

"This is going to be the most requested puppy that you will ever have!"

"Yes! Our family is ready for him!"

"Please consider my friend!"

"Get ready for my application, SSPCA!"

Anyone who was interested in adopting Bueller had only one week to submit their essay and application. Sarah, Jaime, and a few other staffers read through every single submission. There were so many families out there who wanted to love this bulldog. People sent photos and wrote lovely letters explaining how they would accept Bueller into their lives. They described how much love they had to give and why they wanted to give it to Bueller in particular. It was heartwarming to see so many people who wanted to drop everything and care for this dog. How would they possibly decide on one family? By the end of the week, each of them had narrowed down the applications into a handful of their favorites. They compared those favorites, then whittled the pile down even more to the final three options.

"Let's meet with these three families to see who has the best connection with Bueller," Sarah said.

Jaime agreed that it was impossible to make a confident decision without meeting these families and seeing how they interacted with Bueller. And to see how Bueller responded to *them*, too. She was grateful that everyone was willing to take the time to interview the final applicants in person. For Jaime, this whole process had been terrifying and heartbreaking. She had so many questions and fears. Would this new family love Bueller as much as she loved him? Would they spoil him as much as she spoiled him? Would they take care of his medical needs? Should she just keep Bueller because she loved him so much?

Jaime gathered the final three applications into a pile. Bueller's future lay somewhere within her hands. And a wedding photo featuring a white bulldog lay on top.

Lindsey couldn't stop thinking about her adoption application. She had emailed the SSPCA earlier that week to see if they had decided who was adopting Bueller yet. They'd said they hadn't yet because there were so many applications. Since turning in her application two and a half weeks ago, Lindsey had scrolled through all of Bueller's progress on social media. It pulled at her heartstrings to see how hard Bueller was working to get strong. Today, there had been another update on the shelter's page: "Boy, are we exhausted from reading through all of the fabulous applications we received for Bueller! We are narrowing down the field and will start scheduling meetings with our top applicants. We can't wait to celebrate when this guy finds his wonderful new family!"

"They'll probably pick a couple with 2.5 kids who can afford his medical bills because they're doctors or something," Lindsey said to Alex. It was hard to stay optimistic during this process. She knew that so many people wanted Bueller to join their family. What were the odds that Lindsey and Alex would get picked? They were just a regular, everyday couple. They had never had luck like that before—they never had won a contest or a prize. Lindsey scrolled through the comments:

"I would love nothing more than to have him as part of our family!"

"He would be sooo loved!"

"Someone is going to be very lucky to get this beautiful boy!"

"Bueller deserves the best forever home!"

"I've been so anxious waiting to hear back about my application!"

"My family and I are hoping we get to be the lucky family who is picked!"

It was crazy to think that just last month, Lindsey and Alex had been so sad and hopeless about the loss of Chubbs. Now here they were crossing their fingers and toes that a new puppy would come into their lives. But Lindsey knew that they were ready. Just the thought of Bueller napping on their couch or giving them morning kisses warmed her heart. Bueller may have desperately needed a caring new family, but Lindsey and Alex desperately needed a puppy to love. It felt like it was meant to be.

A few days later, Lindsey's phone rang. It was a woman named Sarah from the SSPCA.

It was a Wednesday, just days after Lindsey had gotten the call—the call they had dreamed about! Lindsey and Alex walked up to the front doors of the shelter. They had been asked if they wanted to come by and meet Bueller. Of course they said yes! But they weren't fully celebrating yet. They had a lot of time to think and worry as they sat in traffic on the hour-long drive to Sacramento.

"Do you think another family will walk out when we walk in?" Alex had asked.

Lindsey wasn't sure. But she assumed the shelter was interviewing other people. She was nervous. This was like interviewing for a job, but it was even more important. You could always leave your job, but you could never leave your family. And that's what a pet was—family.

"I'm still in the mindset of 'it's not going to be us,'" she admitted.

As they walked through the front doors, Alex made sure his white button-up shirt was free of wrinkles. Lindsey tugged at her yellow cardigan and adjusted her glasses. They couldn't shake the nerves! But everything moved so quickly as soon as they walked into the SSPCA. They were taken to an office. And then they saw him. It was Bueller! In real life! Not on TV or on social media. Here he was. Lindsey's nerves turned into butterflies. Was this their new dog? It just felt right!

Sarah and Jaime welcomed Lindsey and Alex with a smile. Bueller welcomed them happily, too. Bueller made everyone fall in love with him. And Lindsey and Alex were no exception.

But Jaime was waiting for that spark. That same spark she felt when she first met Bueller. That spark when you just know that a dog was meant for a family and a family was meant for a dog.

"He's so tiny!" Lindsey said. "He's a little ball of wrinkles."

"He's such a meatball," Alex said.

Jaime watched as the couple bent down to greet Bueller. They looked so happy and relieved to finally meet him. Their eyes were sparkling and their gazes were locked on the little pup. Jaime could instantly tell that Lindsey was so nurturing and loving. It was oozing out of her! And she could also see right away that Alex would be a really good doggy dad, just as he had been in the past to Chubbs. She secretly made eye contact with Sarah and gave a smile. This introduction was already going really well.

Jaime and Sarah explained to Lindsey and

Alex that Bueller likely would need surgery somewhere on his leg. They didn't know when or how much it would cost. But it would likely be expensive.

"We'll make it work," Alex said. "We'll save a few bucks every day."

Lindsey nodded. She was watching Bueller scamper around the room. He definitely had a limp and he couldn't fully straighten his legs when he walked, but she was so impressed by his strength.

"We don't care if he has to have one surgery or twenty," Alex added. "We just want to love another dog."

Jaime tried to hide her smile. Sarah was smiling, too. They gave each other another secret head nod. They went on to explain that Bueller still needed constant therapy. Walks, water therapy, leg rubs, and special exercises. Lindsey and

Alex listened carefully and asked smart questions. Jaime liked that this couple was realistic about Bueller's future. They were willing to learn. They wanted to educate themselves. And they had a plan for any medical needs that might come up. Alex explained that they had set up a savings account for Chubbs, who had needed a lot of expensive treatments for his cancer. And Jaime couldn't forget that they had included Chubbs in their wedding photo. It showed that a dog wasn't just a pet, but a part of the family.

Bueller had fun meeting new people. They always were excited to see him and usually got on the floor with him and gave him lots of belly rubs. These people were especially nice. The lady had been sweet talking to Bueller the entire time. The man had a friendly smile with dimples. He picked up Bueller and gave him a hug. Bueller showed him his toys. And he dragged his bed over to the lady to show her. Everyone in the room seemed really happy. Something special was happening. He wasn't sure what, but it just felt right. The other nice ladies grabbed a camera and said, "Say cheese!" Bueller looked right at the camera. In that moment, he felt a spark. Maybe it was the flash of the camera, but maybe it was something else. Something felt different. But now the people were saying good-bye. Wait, where were they going?

Lindsey and Alex walked into the parking lot with their eyes wide and smiles on their faces.

"Did they just ask us if we wanted to take him home?" Lindsey said with a smile. They had asked her and Alex four times if they wanted to take Bueller home *today*. Right now! And each time Lindsey and Alex were in complete shock. They froze. They couldn't believe it. They had been chosen to be Bueller's parents!

Finally, they mustered up the words: "We will absolutely take him home!" But they couldn't take him right this moment. They needed to puppy-proof their house first. Everyone understood. Getting a new puppy was a lifelong commitment. Getting a puppy who required extra care like Bueller did was an even bigger deal.

They had a lot of preparing to do: Where would they do water therapy with him? Where would he sleep? Who would watch him during the day? Did they have enough toys and food? One hundred things were running through Lindsey's mind. Getting a puppy is so much more than, "Oh, he's cute! I want him!" She and Alex were glad the SSPCA didn't sugarcoat anything. The SSPCA worked hard to educate every potential pet owner on what it's really like to care for a pet, and to make sure they were ready to pay for any expensive vet bills in the future.

So were Lindsey and Alex *really* up for all this? Did they have enough money to care for Bueller? Did they have the patience for a puppy? Were they ready to open up their hearts and home to a new family member?

Yes, yes, yes, and yes! It was a no-brainer. As they stepped into their car, Lindsey called the SSPCA. "I just wanted to say again how excited we are to bring Bueller home," Lindsey said as they pulled out of the SSPCA parking lot and headed home. "We'll see you on Friday!" Right now, they had to puppy-proof the house.

The post went up immediately with their first family photo: Bueller, Lindsey, and Alex looking directly at the camera with huge smiles on their faces. "We are so excited to announce that Bueller has found his new family! Alex and Lindsey are newlyweds who lost their beloved bulldog Chubbs to cancer shortly after their wedding. They are ready to welcome a new family member into their lives and are prepared for all the love, snores, and possible medical bills that come along with a special guy like Bueller. They will be coming back later this week to pick him up, and we'll make sure to share his good-byes with all of you. We are over the moon!" The comments came fast.

"He finally has his 'furever' home. So happy for you all!"

"Looks like the perfect match for this very special pup!"

"Bueller is one lucky baby. All the best to Bueller, Alex, and Lindsey!"

"Aww, tears of joy for him."

"It's so heartwarming to see dogs like Bueller get their happily ever after."

Jaime was thrilled that Bueller had found his forever home. There was no doubt in her mind that Lindsey and Alex were the perfect family for this special bulldog. Things couldn't have worked out any better. But she couldn't help but feel crushed knowing that by Friday morning, Bueller would no longer be hers.

CHAPTER 7

THE BIG DAY

IT WAS LIKE CHRISTMAS EVE. LINDSEY couldn't sleep. Tomorrow was going to be one of the best. Days. Ever.

Today had been crazy. She and Alex had frantically prepared their house for a new puppy. It had been a long time since they had to worry about potty training and keeping a little pup out of trouble around the house.

They had potty pads on the floor. They had a bed. They had food. And a crate. Plenty of toys. They added a rug to any slippery surfaces so it would be easier for Bueller to walk. The backyard was ready with a green glow-in-the-dark ball they could throw for Bueller to keep his muscles moving. Lindsey and Alex had learned how to massage and stretch the puppy's legs. Their neighbors had even said Bueller could come over any time to do water therapy exercises in their pool. The neighbors had a goofy but loveable rottweiler named Nibbles who would hopefully become one of Bueller's first dog friends. But Lindsey was thinking too far ahead. First, they had to bring Bueller home and get used to being a new family of three.

The day was finally here. It was Friday morning. Time to adopt Bueller. In just a few hours, Bueller would be sitting in their living room. The three of them would be together at last. Lindsey and Alex could hardly contain their excitement. Just as they were about to leave the house, they got a call from Sarah: "Just so you know, a few local news outlets are going to be there filming everything." Uh-oh. Lindsey had taken off work, but Alex couldn't. So he had lied and called in sick to work. He didn't want to miss this moment! However, he couldn't be seen on live TV when he had just told his boss he was staying home because he didn't feel well!

What would they do now? Lindsey didn't want to go by herself, especially with a news crew there. And she wanted someone else to drive so she could hold Bueller in her lap on the way home in case he was nervous. It was an exciting day, but it was also overwhelming and a little nerve-racking. Alex thought fast—he called his dad, and his dad agreed to go to the SSPCA with Lindsey. Phew! Alex was disappointed to be missing the first moments with Bueller, but he knew that Lindsey would bring Bueller home as quickly as she could. The three of them would be reunited eventually. It would just happen at their house now instead of at the SSPCA.

As Lindsey drove to the SSPCA with her father-in-law, she had plenty of time to start worrying. She had been nervous before, but now she was even more nervous. *Is Bueller going to like me? Is he going to like living with us? Is he going to feel welcomed into our family?* She thought of the past few weeks and how many times she had watched videos of Bueller and studied his progress. She thought of their meeting just two days ago and how well it went. She thought of all the work she and Alex had done over the past twenty-four hours to prepare their house for Bueller. And then she thought of all the love they had given to Chubbs for nine years. That made her feel better. *Chubbs had a great life with us. And Bueller will, too,* she told herself.

Everyone who worked at the shelter had fallen in love with Bueller over the past two months. The best part of Dr. Laurie's job was seeing a sick or injured animal get better and get adopted. She was always so impressed by the families who came into the shelter and happily adopted all sorts of animals—old, young, injured, funny-looking—and loved them for the rest of their lives. She was especially proud of the work they had done for Bueller. *Lindsey and Alex are going to love him to death just as he is,* she told herself. But it was still sad to see him go.

Jaime gave Bueller one last kiss good-bye as she handed him over to Sarah.

"Are you sure?" Sarah asked.

"No one wants to see a snot-bubbling person crying," Jaime said. "I'm kind of a coward."

She had decided to hide from the cameras. It was better if she didn't see Bueller get handed over to Lindsey. She wouldn't be able to stop crying. Was it possible for a heart to be broken but happy at the same time? She knew Lindsey and Alex were Bueller's forever family. She couldn't have dreamed of a better home for him. But her own home would feel so empty tonight without Bueller in it.

Bueller wasn't sure why, but there was a lot of excitement in the air. A news crew had filmed him walking around the front lobby this morning. After that, all of the nice people he had met over the past two months came by and gave him hugs and kisses. Some of them cried. Then more cameras and reporters had arrived. They clapped and cheered for Bueller, especially when he walked. They gave him treats! And then things got a little quieter. Something big was about to happen; Bueller just didn't know what. But he was ready.

Three different news teams with big cameras and microphones were waiting inside.

"Tell us your thoughts!"

"Do you have any worries?"

"Do you want to sit down?"

Whoa. Lindsey was overwhelmed by all the attention as she walked through the front doors of the SSPCA. She hadn't been prepared for all of these interviews. Bueller was so popular, though, so she shouldn't have been surprised. A lot of people had wanted to give their love to this little four-month-old pup. And she was the lucky one who had been chosen to take him home. As she started talking to the reporters, one of the staffers came around the corner. In her arms was a brown bulldog wearing a bright green bandanna. Before Lindsey knew it, Bueller was sitting in her lap.

"Hi, handsome! Hi, baby!" She gave him a hug and a kiss. His little face. His little belly. He seemed nervous, just like Lindsey was. But she couldn't wait to start a new life with Bueller in it. He was hers, and she was his. She had almost forgotten the cameras were there until the reporters started asking more questions.

"It was love at first sight," Lindsey said into the cameras. "We just have so much love to give."

She told them about how strong Bueller was and how excited she and Alex were to have him join their family. Then it was time to go. With a folder of information in her hand, she and Bueller walked out of the building and into the March sun. It was time to go home.

So this was what everyone had been preparing for today. What a great surprise! Bueller loved car rides. Right now he was sitting on a white blanket in the lap of the nice lady he had met a couple days ago. She had come back to get him! And now they were stepping out of the car and walking into a new house. Hey, the nice man with the big smile was here! Awesome! They were hugging him and crying. Bueller gave them kisses. *Don't cry, I'm here!* he thought. The last home he had been in was wonderful. And he knew this one would be, too.

"This is the greatest thing ever," Lindsey said to Alex. "We hit the jackpot."

They were both just staring at Bueller, admiring him. Bueller was rolling on the floor and loving his new toys, especially the green glow-in-the-dark ball. He had the cutest, tiniest bark. And it was so funny when he stuck his tongue out. It felt like they had just brought a new baby home from the hospital. Their friends and family couldn't wait to stop by and meet the newest addition to the family. Lindsey's twin sister was planning on coming over right away.

"We'll still cry about Chubbs, and he's still

in our hearts," Lindsey said. "He did all he could, and we did all we could."

"But if we never had Chubbs, we would never have met Bueller," Alex said, smiling. "Some things are just meant to be."

Lindsey agreed, thinking back to the moment her heart melted when she first saw Bueller's sweet face on TV. "He was our dog from the start."

They said a silent thank-you to Chubbs and gave Bueller a big hug.

CHAPTER 8

EPILOGUE

"HEY, IT'S BUELLER!"

It had been two years since Lindsey and Alex adopted Bueller. They were used to getting stopped at the dog park by people who recognized their famous bulldog. Lindsey had been posting updates online so Bueller's fans and everyone at the SSPCA could continue to follow along on his journey.

If people at the dog park didn't recognize Bueller, they would often ask, "Oh no, what happened?" when they saw him limping around. Lindsey and Alex would explain what swimmer syndrome was and how far Bueller had come. There was nothing to be sad about—Bueller was an inspiration!

Bueller was such a brave fighter and he never gave up. Since they adopted him, Bueller had become a stronger, more confident dog. And he had brought smiles to so many people. Lindsey got messages from people from the Philippines, from Europe, and from all over the world about how Bueller had brightened their day and helped them get through tough times.

Alex and Lindsey felt like every conversation they had with people they met in the park or online was a light that could guide others to adopting a special-needs pet. They liked to tell people, "Every adoptable dog has their own story, but also a family that is perfect for them." They knew that adopting a special-needs dog changed you and made you think differently about pet adoption. Just because these animals are different, that doesn't make them any less loving. Alex and Lindsey had learned that first-hand. And that's why Kobe had joined their family a year after Bueller did.

Kobe was a three-year-old French bulldog who was deaf and blind in one eye. They gave him the nickname "Shadow" because he followed Bueller everywhere. Bueller and Kobe were best friends. When Kobe had needed surgery on his eye, Bueller went to the vet with him for support. They liked to say that Bueller was Kobe's therapy dog.

Bueller ran around the dog park and Kobe followed as usual.

"He's a little force to be reckoned with," Lindsey said to Alex.

The running lasted about two minutes before Bueller needed a rest.

"Sure, he'll take a nap along the way here and there," she added with a laugh. "But he's full of life!"

Bueller was doing great, but Lindsey and Alex always had to be careful that he didn't hurt himself by running too long or jumping too high. They always picked Bueller up to put him in the car or onto the bed or couch. And they used to push him around in a stroller for long walks—until he grew out of it. He was forty-five pounds now. A forty-five-pound lap dog! Now they rolled the bulldog around in a red wagon. When they added an umbrella and a fan to the wagon, Bueller couldn't have been happier.

With both Bueller and Kobe, Lindsey and Alex had taken a chance. It was a risk. These dogs needed extra love, physical therapy, and surgeries. But Alex and Lindsey couldn't have been happier with their little family. They worked hard taking care of these dogs, and their hard work paid off. Every time Kobe gave them slobbery bulldog kisses. Every time Bueller laid his head on Lindsey's hand while she ate breakfast and gave her the sweetest face ever, begging for just one bite. Every time Kobe rested for hours on the couch next to Bueller, even when Bueller had been the one recovering from a surgery, not Kobe.

"Come on," Alex called to Bueller. Bueller ran over as fast as his little legs would carry him.

"Wait for your brother," Lindsey said. Kobe always kept more of a slow and steady pace.

Alex picked up Bueller, and Lindsey scooped Kobe into her arms. The family of four walked home smiling. Two dogs were in their arms, and another was in their hearts.

DEALING WITH THE LOSS OF A PET

Lindsey and Alex lost their first dog, Chubbs, to cancer. They felt sad for months, but they eventually overcame their sadness and now love to talk about all of the happy memories they shared with Chubbs. Everyone deals with the loss of a pet differently, but Lindsey has some advice for how she worked through losing her dog.

1. KNOW THAT IT'S NOT EASY.

"It's heartbreaking, and it might be hard for a long time," Lindsey says. "It's important to know you aren't alone, and it's okay to feel the way you do. To feel sad, or any other type of emotion, is okay. It's important to grieve and to express your feelings."

2. SHARE YOUR LOVE.

"Honor your pet," Lindsey says. "They were a part of your family for so long. Sometimes a pet is your best friend. Sometimes they are the first ones to greet you in the morning and when you come home from school. It's important to talk about all of the amazing memories you have of them and share them with your family and friends."

3. REMEMBER THEM.

"My dog Chubbs loved the beach," she says. "He would run in the sand and sniff the salty air. He could stay there forever and play. Now when we visit the beach, we look for things there that remind us of him. Remembering the happy times you had with your pet is the best part of it all. You will have those memories forever. They will always be with you in your heart."

ADOPTING SPECIAL-NEEDS PETS

Adopting a pet from a shelter is a great way to help out the animal community. And there are so many homeless animals who need someone to care for them. According to the ASPCA, about 6.5 million pets (mostly dogs and cats) enter animal shelters in the United States every year. Only 3.2 million of those animals go on to get adopted and find forever homes.

Animal shelters take in pets from all sorts of backgrounds. Some pets are found abandoned and brought in by a stranger, while others are surrendered by owners who can't care for them anymore. Unfortunately, it can be harder for pets with special needs to get adopted because they may require extra work. But Alex and Lindsey believe special-needs pets can teach an important life lesson: "Just because you're different doesn't make you any better or worse." They have a few tips for anyone who is considering adopting a special-needs pet.

1. BE ACCEPTING AND OPEN.

An animal may need surgery, physical therapy sessions to help him get stronger, or constant extra care like Kobe, who's deaf and partially blind. "When you work hard helping out these animals, the benefit is just unspeakable," Alex says. You could make a big difference in the life of this animal—and they could make one in yours, too!

2. DO YOUR RESEARCH.

Take getting a pet seriously. Learn more about the kind of animal you are adopting. What does that pet need and how do they usually behave? Learn as much as you can about any difficulties your pet may have to overcome. Lindsey and Alex hadn't heard of swimmer syndrome before they met Bueller. But they learned what they were getting into by doing research online before they adopted him and asking the vet a lot of questions.

3. SAVE UP.

Pets can be expensive, especially if they need surgeries or extra medical care to help them live a more comfortable life. Lindsey and Alex started a savings account for their pets. But some shelters may be willing to help cover the costs of an animal's surgery or shots. Gather as much information as possible so you can save enough money in advance.

4. PREPARE YOUR HOME.

For dogs with swimmer syndrome, slippery floors can be dangerous, because it makes it even more difficult for them to stand with their legs directly below their body. So Lindsey and Alex added rugs to the hardwood and tile floors in their home. Little changes like these can make a big difference in the health of your new pet. Talk to the vet about what changes you can make in your own home to keep your new pet safe and happy.

Shelters try to take care of animals no matter what issues they are facing. They give each pet a medical checkup, shots, and a treatment plan before they put them up for adoption. The shelter will provide as much information as possible to the new owners about their pet's medical history as well as their likes and dislikes, and any interesting personality traits. Check your local humane society or SPCA for pets who are available for adoption in your area. Maybe you can change an animal's life, just like Lindsey and Alex did!